Have a Great One!

A Homeless Man's Story

J. C. Simmons, Wyandanch High School

By Laurie Anthony

Have A Great One!
A Homeless Man's Story

Copyright ©1999 by Laurie Anthony

Published by:
Anthony Publishing
P.O. Box 3522
Dublin, OH 43016-0259
614-798-9337
lanthony5@aol.com

ISBN: 0-9675298-0-8

Printed in the U.S.A. by Morris Publishing
3212 East Hwy 30 *Kearney, NE 68847* 1-800-650-7888

Dedication

This book is dedicated to Mamie Simmons, who, in spite of everything, was loved and cherished.

Acknowledgments

I want to express my thanks to all my colleagues who have helped me with their constructive feedback and editing suggestions, especially Jeanne Newman, Juli Keifer, Gretchen Crawford, Connie Rush, Virginia Forsythe, Carol Homon, and Louise Borden.

I especially want to thank J.C. Simmons, Jeff Simmons, and Mechell Simmons for their willingness to spend time with me and for their openness and confidence.

My deepest thanks to my husband, T.J. for his relentless support and encouragement and for the hours he spent helping me revise and edit my manuscript.

I especially want to thank my son, Joey, for first planting the seed.

Contents

Everyone Has Gotta Start Somewhere

Everyone has gotta start somewhere
So why not let it be now
The truth is in every one of us
And everyone wants to feel proud
Life is not a joke
Life is not a game
No one goes through life
Without feeling a little pain
Just like happiness is for those who seek
Sadness comes with defeat
But we should not walk around
With our heads hangin' down
Because a frown is really a smile
Turned upside down
So whatever you want to do
You should know it's up to you
And whatever you want to be
It shall be plain for you to see
That life was made for you
Just as well as it was made for me.

Strive to do your best
And let God do the rest!

Willie G.
The Poet of Central Park

A moment's insight is sometimes worth a life's experience.
Oliver Wendall Holmes, Sr.

Introduction

"I could never live in New York City! A weekend there is just enough for me!" I adamantly spoke loudly and clearly to my fourteen-year old son, Joey, whose dream was to go to the city and perform on Broadway. We had spent many weekends in New York since we first introduced him to leather-painted boots from the village and the roller-blading musical "Starlight Express" when he was six years old. The city's neon flashing lights, reverberating horns and screeching brakes always merged together like a fourth of July fireworks display and made my nerve endings twitch and contract. After a few days of feeling like I was in a drug-induced state, I yearned for the motionless quiet of Ohio. "It's so hectic and so overwhelming." I continued. "Now tell me honestly, can you see me there? As much as I like peace and quiet?"

Joey shrugged his shoulders, having been in this conversation with my husband, T.J. and I many times. We were very comfortable living in Dublin, an affluent suburb of Columbus in our home overlooking a creek that stormed forcefully from the spring rains and trickled slightly in the summer. The neighborhood sat away from the busy roads like a weekend retreat getaway. And we had four dogs. Four animals that would not make a move to New York under any conditions. But Joey didn't give up; he just kept pleading with us. He wanted to live in New York.

A fourteen-year old with such a monumental dream! Joey began acting and singing as a young child and devoted all his time to the participation and appreciation of the theater and music. The theater opportunities in Columbus couldn't compare to those in New York City. Maybe we could spend a week or two in the city in the summer, I compromised, to see what it was like and hopefully Joey would get a few auditions.

2

Joey was a typical only child. Along with being independent, self-directed and somewhat self-centered, he was overindulged by us. Greatly. Hearing "no" from us was an infrequent occurrence. Yet, in spite of our overindulgence, we hoped he felt loved and valued, and confident in himself and his abilities. That's all we really wanted for our child--to have high self-esteem.

It wasn't surprising, then, that his dreams rose far above other kids his age. He was used to dreaming for the improbable and never letting up.

This could be a wonderful opportunity for Joey, I thought, but it had to be more than that, for all of us to pick up and move there. It had to be a joint decision or resentment would follow us there like a stray dog. After a few months of discussing the possibilities with my husband, "I'll never move to New York" changed to "I think it would be a wonderful adventure!" It's amazing how everything you are so set against transforms itself like the sky after a storm when your outlook changes.

Opportunity for Joey? Yes. Opportunity for my husband and me? Maybe . . . maybe. Living in Manhattan for a year would be an experience that most forty-something folks would not undertake. I would take a year's leave of absence from my teaching job; this alone was an inviting prospect. Time to myself, time to read, write and exercise. We'd move beyond the theater district and explore the city with an open agenda. We'd have the time to bond as a family and for my husband and me to bond as a couple.

We did it. One year. Joey would attend the Professional Performing Arts High School, T.J. would work in Columbus and New York, and I was, well, let's just say I was in heaven!

We packed up our van and drove to New York. It was quite a complicated ordeal--we had to find someone to stay in our house and watch our dogs. And finding an apartment in New York was not so easy. Rents were sky-high and we wanted a place where we would feel safe and secure. But everything worked out smoothly for us, as if it was all just meant to be.

Once we got settled in, I was anxious to get outside and explore the city. Many tourists filled Times Square, delighting in the theater billboards and flashing lights. The nostalgic Greenwich Village lured me into coffee shops and outdoor cafes; the cool breeze off the river at Battery Park motioned me to the Statue of Liberty and Ellis Island. I captured New York's ambiance by carefully following my maps. Little did I know that my New York experience would open up doors that weren't listed in the pages of my tourist guidebook.

There was always something to do here. I had whole days before me, just waiting to be filled. I relished this time. Walking along Broadway in the August steam felt like being covered by a woolen blanket with holes that let in the night air. Lights and sounds furled my senses like an ice-cream headache—it hurt momentarily but soon passed. Once I moved beyond the tourist souvenir shops, I found vendors selling old books and magazines and fruit stands with bargain prices.. Bouquets of flowers colored the sidewalks with an open invitation to partake and the aroma of flavored coffees mellowed my steps.

I found numerous places to sit--in Bryant Park amidst the lunchtimers and chess players, atrium areas between buildings, and even the endless church steps at St. Patrick's Cathedral when my feet absolutely needed a break. I enjoyed walking more than anything else and left early in the morning to explore the hidden bridges and open fields in Central Park. I'd find a bench where I could sit and write, somewhere that was frequented by others for safety reasons. But sitting high on the rocks or under an ancient tree was more conducive to my need for reflection.

No matter where I sat, there were always people to watch, conversations to overhear and food to be bought. The myriad of people here was truly the melting pot I had learned about in school. Business people, joggers, dog-walkers, tourists, shoppers, artists, construction workers, city workers, dancers in their tights, teenagers moving in groups on skateboards, bicycle delivery men, vendors, and the shoes. The diversity of the city was in the shoes. Platforms, spiked heels, tennis shoes, winged-tipped, shiny black shoes, hiking boots, open-toe sandals, clogs, backless heels, Doc Martins, Sketchers, knee-high leather boots, and Birkenstocks. For each pair of shoes there was a hairstyle to match. The many hairstyles and hair

4

colors reflected the city's diversity of age, color and personality, from the reddish-black streaked hair to the thick braided plaits extending down backs.

I tried to be careful, in my own sort of naïve way. All the things I had heard about New York accompanied me as I walked around exploring the shops and cafes, but I soon began to weave in and out of the crowd as I picked up my pace. I'm starting to blend in, I thought, the first time someone stopped and asked me for directions. My attire became more casual and I stored my makeup away. I didn't need to worry about how I looked here. In New York, it didn't matter. Anything and everything was acceptable. It was easy to just be myself.

Early in the morning, the benches in the park were covered with bodies in blankets and coats, with paper bags and cans on the ground around them. The homeless. One man was pulling down his pants next to a tree to relieve himself; another man was searching through a trashcan. If I stopped and sat down, someone would always approach me and ask for money or food. It was as if I wore a sign on my face that said, "Ask me, I won't say no." Perhaps it was the relaxed way that I sat, or my open journal or book, or my informal attire. My husband said my face told all--even behind sunglasses I wore an open invitation.

First, I left food on benches--fresh bagels, donuts, juice, and coffee. I knew someone would appreciate it. Then I got bolder and started talking to homeless people that approached me and asked for some money or food. I watched one young woman move down the path slowly, her cerebral palsy making the task of lifting her bag cumbersome. She sat down and breathed a heavy sigh and my heart went out to her. I decided to approach her. Her name was Linda; she was thirty-four years old. She told me her story-- how she was trying to save enough money for bus fare to get back home to Minnesota. She had $1000 once, but it was stolen and now panhandled on Fifth Avenue in front of the church. A good place there, she said, people very generous to her. It was hard for me to keep sitting there; her unpleasant body odor reached my nostrils and I had to keep turning my face away. She talked easily as I asked her questions and I knew

5

she just needed someone to listen to her. She said her family threw her out because she couldn't get a job. When she said she planned to get a job at MTV, I knew she was out of touch with reality. I wanted to give her money for bus fare but I didn't. I wished her luck and I walked away. I felt torn inside, wishing I could help her yet knowing there wasn't much I could do. A social service agency needed to find her and hook her up with the appropriate services. She shouldn't be on the streets—not with her physical disability and emotional problems.

I want to learn more about the homeless, I thought, and I went back to my bench and wrote in my journal, "I want to help a homeless person." There was no doubt in my mind. I was drawn to the listless faces and saw their pain, pain measured in degrees by the heaviness of the eyelids. Even when I was young, I was sensitive to the pain of others. When I started teaching, I found myself drawn to the kids who had problems. I remember a parent saying I was the first teacher who ever liked her son! And I thought, what a terrible thing for a child to go to school and not feel loved. Over the years, I had my students collect clothes and food for the needy. One year I worked with an agency and arranged for my class to clean and furnish a home for a homeless family. Now here I was in New York City, and the plight of the homeless still drew me in and their faces followed me home.

> You are blessed as long as you view what happens as a blessing.
> *Unknown*

1 Out of the Blue

I pushed the door of my apartment open and merged into the movement of people on the busy sidewalks walking purposely ahead, no eyes meeting, no smiles shared. The warm breeze touched my cheeks and moved me along. The sounds of the city fell like hail from the sky and I knew I was far from home.

The city had a way of waking me up in the morning in spite of my dark sunglasses and slow-moving feet. I approached the corner of Seventh Avenue and 57th Street where the subways rolled people onto the sidewalk with the urgency of a rising tide.

I noticed the cups before I saw him. The cups were fast-food discards, about a dozen of them, stacked on top of one another. My eyes moved to a plastic Pepsi bottle at the bottom of the stack that was filled with coins. A man sat against the wall of Carnegie Hall on a plastic mail bin, holding up these cups as if building a tower. White-gray curls hung over his ears, wisps of his Santa-like beard insulated his face and wide piano teeth yellowed with age complimented his dark skin. I slowed down and watched him greet people with the politeness of a Disney World guide as they put money into the top cup and watched it fall to the bottom. There was something inviting about this man's smile, and although he was dressed the part, he just didn't seem like the other homeless people I'd seen.

After only a couple of weeks in the city, I was already forming a daily routine of sorts. I adjusted my backpack and headed toward the park. It was only a few blocks away but I did a lot of maneuvering through New Yorkers who were oblivious to a wide-eyed tourist trying to jump into the flow of movement on the streets.

The beeping cabs and blaring horns faded into the distance as I turned into Central Park. I shifted into another level of consciousness and my feet slowed down by an empty bench. I like it here, I thought, the sun sending fine lines of light through the trees and resting on my face. My books, my journal, my coffee and muffin fell into place by my side and a still quiet hung like a tarp overhead.

Not all the benches were all empty. I noticed feet moving beneath an old army-green blanket. I breathed in a cloud of alcohol-scented air and suddenly a loud belch brought a woman upright on the bench. She scratched her head and rubbed her eyes. I jumped, more out of curiosity than fear, noticing her hair wild around her head, her cheeks wrinkled like walnuts and her caked-dry eyes. I looked away but my brain registered the sights and sounds I tried not to see. Someone sat down on another bench and blocked my view but I could still see inside this homeless woman, this woman with sandstone eyes.

I recalled a time when we were in New York years ago. Joey was very young and we had just come out of a play. We walked by a homeless man asking for change. Joey had asked me, "How could you just walk by him?" I searched for an answer--I didn't know why the American work ethic was valued more than simple compassion. It was no accident that we were back again in New York City, ten years after my son's poignant question.

I finished my coffee and took a long walk along the park before I headed home. The hot sun peered over the buildings and a steam from the pavement colored the air. As I approached 57th Street, I noticed the cups again above the heads in front of me and watched the man with the cups drinking the last of a bottle of water. He started getting his bags together and noticed me glancing at him. "Have a great day," he said. I smiled and walked on and felt his eyes following me. I stopped at the sidewalk vendor and walked back to him. "Here's some lunch for you." I smiled slightly. "Just a bagel and some coffee."

"Thank you kindly. I was just going to get something to eat." He tipped his hat at me, his smile pointing upward toward his cocoa eyes. The breeze lifted my steps as I walked home.

He's approachable, I thought, not like other homeless people I'd seen. His appearance was neat and clean and he was so polite. I decided I'd bring him another bagel the next time I saw him.

Saturday morning. The summer sun eased between the buildings casting a faint glow on the morning streets. The man with the cups wasn't on the corner. I wonder if he moved on, I thought, feeling a little disappointed because I had gotten him some breakfast at the deli, but mostly because I was looking forward to seeing him.

I went to the park for my morning walk and the taste of the morning mist worked its way through my body. I felt my body relax and my thoughts popped up and rolled around in my mind with the surge of a breath mint. I kept thinking about my homeless friend. Although I had always gotten advice like, "Don't give money, don't make eye contact, and watch your purse," I just had this feeling that he was different somehow. His image lingered in my mind like a movie you want to rewind and watch over and over again. I wondered how he became homeless and how hard winters must be for him.

Many of my evenings were a contrast to my mornings. My husband and I would go to a play or out to dinner, but now I was sure to box up any leftovers and leave them in the park. I felt a little guilty about the luxuries I had in my life--having a car that we left sitting in our garage in Ohio, having a closet full of clothes that I didn't need, and living in a fancy apartment in New York. My life was so easy, yet I had worked hard to get where I was. I didn't know what it was like to be homeless, but I knew what it was like to live on a budget. I grew up in a large family. My dad worked long hours and my mother worked as well. Although I didn't feel poor, I knew that money wasn't readily available. I remember how excited I'd be just to get my sister's hand-me-downs or to eat a McDonald's hamburger. But I had the opportunity to change my lifestyle because of my parent's strong work ethic and belief in education.

A few days later I saw my friend on the corner as I crossed the street. He's back, I thought, and I was glad I had stopped to get him some breakfast.

"Hello there. Here's some breakfast. Oh, how do you like your coffee?"

He adjusted his cap and his sunglasses moved off his nose. "Any way I can get it," he said, pushing his sunglasses back in place. He smiled with the ease of a child.

"I'm Laurie." My voice was light and upbeat. I held out my hand.

"I'm J.C. It's a pleasure to meet you, Laurie." His voice rolled out like musical notes.

I asked him if J.C. stood for Jesus Christ and he laughed, saying no, it stood for James and Clinton, like the president. My gaze fell on the cups and I fumbled for some change in my pocket, recognizing that this was his trademark. I put it in the top cup and watched it fall to the next and the next until it landed in the plastic bottle on the bottom. "That's pretty neat. How did you ever think of doing this, J.C.?"

"Well, it just kind of happened. I didn't plan it." He sat up straight, proudly holding the cups out high in front of him. "I used to just have a few cups to sort coins in, to keep myself organized. After sitting out here in all kinds of weather, the bottoms of the cups started to wear through so I started stacking them and the coins fell to the bottom. Kids love them the most," he said with a crooked grin, "but even adults like watching the coins fall to the bottom."

And sure enough, as he spoke, a woman lifted her daughter up to put some coins in the top cup. "Thank you kindly, little Isabelle." J.C. caught her eyes and her face lit up as she heard the clink of coins fall to the bottom. "You have a great day now."

I was surprised that J.C. knew her name. He looked at me as if anticipating my question. "I know lots of people here by name. I knew Isabelle long before she was even born." He grinned to see if I understood what he was saying.

My lips turned up slightly as I thought Isabelle must be about two or three. "I guess you've been here awhile, J.C?"

"For four years, four long years. Almost five, actually."

I thought about the past four years of my life and couldn't imagine how his life must have been during that time. I wanted to ask him some more questions, but someone else came up and started talking to him. "I'll see you tomorrow, okay?"

He raised his hand in acknowledgment as I walked away. "Have a great one."

The next day he continued talking about the cups, as if he just remembered we hadn't finished our conversation. He pointed to the writing on the top cup. "I select my cups carefully. Restaurant owners notice if I have their cups and they seem to appreciate the free advertising." He continued to talk earnestly. "You'd be surprised how many people take pictures of me and my cups. They ask me about them, just like you, sometimes wanting to buy them from me." His animated face resembled a cartoon character. "One woman offered me fifty dollars for my cups, said they were a work of sculpture and of course, I couldn't turn her down!"

I laughed, thinking that only in New York would this happen.

He leaned forward and held out the cups to a person slowing down. I gave him a puzzled look, thinking he was being kind of forward. He noticed my face and explained, "I try to make it as easy as I can for my regular customers." His smile was as mischievous as a child eating candy. "Now only the regular ones get this kind of service!" he added.

Regular customers? He talked as if he was operating a business. But whoever heard of a panhandling business? His stories could be part of a circus act, I thought. I stood there and watched him for awhile, amazed by the slight smiles forming on the faces of people passing him by, the fleeting glimmer in eyes and the slowing down of footsteps. His presence captivated the most unsuspecting pedestrians to turn their heads. I wasn't alone in noticing him— everyone else did too.

I felt comfortable talking to him and my apprehension about homeless people seemed to dissipate. He had a way of putting me at ease, as if he had invited me over for tea. Since I started going over to the park, I had had several encounters with homeless people. At Columbus Circle, I noticed a gray-haired woman conversing with her outstretched leashed dogs. She delivered coos and caahs to them yet her face ached of wanting more recognition than her dogs could give her. A tenacious, robust homeless woman must have noticed her the same time as I did and volunteered, "Your dogs are so cute!" in a high and spirited voice. The old woman's face lit up. This woman finally has a chance to talk about her dogs, her life, I thought. And who takes the time to ask her—a homeless person!

But another time I was sitting on a bench, very intent in my writing and not aware of what was going on around me. I was jarred into awareness when an old, scraggly-looking man approached the bench and sat down close to me. He spoke loudly into my ear, "Write hockey stick." I shook my head, not even looking at him and just continued to write. I was involved in my writing and was just hoping he'd realize that and leave. "Write hockey stick," he demanded even louder. I shook my head. Finally he yelled, "What the hell is wrong with hockey stick?" I looked at him, suddenly aware of his presence. My gut registered an impending danger so I quickly packed my things together and left without looking back.[1]

That evening my thoughts were unsettling. On one hand I felt very compassionate and on the other hand I felt afraid. The "hockey stick" man had frightened me and I knew I should be more cognizant of my surroundings. J.C.'s warm demeanor and unobtrusive manner felt unthreatening to me, but I had to remember that he still was a stranger to me in a city I didn't know. I fell asleep, knowing I wanted to understand how and why he became homeless.

> Everyone must row with the oars he has.
> *English Proverb*

2 First Clues

The summer days passed by quickly. I stopped and talked to J.C. several mornings a week. It was this way that our relationship developed, conversations overlapping like a carefully woven basket. It's easy to begin feeling responsible for something once you start taking care of it, like a stray cat that comes to your door each morning. That's how it was with J.C. and me. I made an unspoken commitment to him, bringing him breakfast with the regularity of mail delivery. He would watch for me to walk down that block with anticipation and delight, always welcoming me with a "Hello Lady Laurie" smile. My commitment of food became one of time-- stretches of time that opened me to his heart. He needed to talk and I wanted to listen. It seemed like such as easy thing; something I had the time, the energy and the motivation to do.

I'd stand with him sometimes for an hour or so and listen to his stories and comments, always amazed at how knowledgeable he was about current events. "I listen to the radio all the time," he said, "so I can keep up with what's going on in the world. Just ask me, I know." And he was right about that. Sometimes I'd look through the newspaper and sure enough, there was the story in the news!

Depending on the time of day, I'd see different people stop by. He knew many people by name; some put money in his cups and others just shook his hand and placed a dollar or two in his grasp. I'd lean back against the wall and watch, taking it all in. I had to laugh when a woman that J.C. called "Miss Dimples" put some change in the cups and then came back and added more. She smiled as she said, "This thing is taking all my money."

J.C. sat there like a magician casting a spell. He was a fixture that had been working properly for years without any upkeep; his own station set up like an office of sorts. People moved by him and smiled and nodded, some stopping and shaking his hand. Policemen waved to him, delivery trucks pulled over to the curb, and sometimes someone would hop out of the truck and drop off a package of food for him. Dogs wagged their tails as they approached him and J.C. knew them all by name. Children in strollers would turn their heads as far back as they could to keep him in view as they were pushed along the sidewalk. His endearing smile and laughter definitely mesmerized many!

My friendship with J.C. made me more curious about homelessness. The library was always a second home to me so I found it easily. I always devoured books on whatever it was that was going on in my life at that time. Now I wanted to find out more about homelessness. Once I settled in at the appropriate branch, I pulled books and journals off the shelves and found the numbers shocking-- over 700,000 people were homeless nationally and over 40,000 in New York City alone.[2] Many of the homeless just stayed with friends or family, however, so estimates varied.[3]

Many homeless people had no one to look out for them; they were isolated from family members and friends, many times of their own choice. They were loners with low self-esteem, frequently depressed and distrustful. Many had psychological problems and health concerns--the list went on and on. Some characteristics resulted in the homelessness; some of them became more pronounced after becoming homeless.[4]

As I perused the streets, I noticed that some homeless people were quiet; some talked to others or just to themselves. Usually they carried several bags or pushed a cart. Some sat on corners or on benches; some slept on cardboard in doorways. Most seemed invisible to the people walking by who didn't acknowledge them even when spoken to.

J.C. didn't fit into this picture--at least not completely. He was one of the most upbeat persons I saw throughout the day--far from being depressed. He also seemed to feel pretty good about himself-- actually had somewhat of an inflated ego. I wondered if J.C. was educated or had any work experience. There had to be something he could do besides beg on the street corner, given his personality and intelligence. It just didn't make sense to me.

I wondered where our compassion was and why was there such a large gap between the haves and have nots.[5] So much depended upon how one was raised and educated and even then, there were no guarantees. Anyone could become homeless. The data attributed homelessness to unemployment, mental illness, or substance abuse and 22% were veterans.[6] I wasn't surprised at what I read, but wondered how often mental problems or substance abuse was the result of homelessness.[7] And although one in five homeless persons had jobs, they remained homeless. It was more complicated than the data showed.[8]

I always believed that one person could make a difference in the life of another. When I was young, my Auntie Ann and Uncle Johnny treated me like I was a star, in spite of my gangly appearance and introvertedness. It was a self-fulfilling prophecy--when treated with high expectations and faith, I began to believe in myself. I was in a position now to be on the giving rather than the receiving end. I was comfortable with my commitment to J.C.

One morning while talking with J.C., a cheerful voice caught my attention.

"Hey, J.C. You gotta get out of this rain."

"Hello there, Helen of Troy!" He took off his hat, and shook the water off of it. "Oh, I'm used to it. Gotta be, in my line of work."

"You need someone to take care of you." Helen was a slender, attractive dark-haired woman who winked at J.C. as she talked. And she seemed to enjoy teasing him.

"Now don't you worry about me. I've made a lot of friends sitting here and everyone looks out for me." His chapped hands gestured in a charade-like manner. "But you go on now, you don't want to get sick."

"Well, everyone sure appreciates what you've added to this corner." Helen looked at him intently and gave him a dollar bill before she walked away. "See you tomorrow."

J.C. put the dollar into his zippered jacket pocket. As he talked with Helen, he didn't stop greeting others. "Hello there. Have a great

Buckeye Day," he said to a man sporting an Ohio State sweatshirt who called J.C. "Mr. Cupman." He seemed to have a nickname for people and I wondered what mine would be.

J.C.'s sense of humor never failed to amaze me. "You know what they say, to get to Carnegie Hall, it's practice, practice, practice." His voice quavered gently. "And to stay out here, it's endurance, endurance, endurance!"

He motioned to a woman jogging by. "That's one of my former students." He saw the look on my face. "I was a teacher you know, right down at Seventh and 24th--the Fashion Industry School."

A teacher, I thought, and started to ask him to tell me more, this really being the first clue I'd gotten about his past. But J.C. didn't miss a beat and continued to greet people. When it finally started to slow down, he pulled out one of the stuffed plastic bags behind him. "Look at this." He held up a pair of polyester brown-striped pants. "Brand new. Still has the tags." I moved my eyes toward the bag and noticed the other clothes in there. Everything so neat and orderly, like him. He dressed in layers; a heavy sweater over a tee shirt today, and other days wore a plaid shirt that looked like it came straight from Bloomingdales.

"You have some nice clothes, J.C." I touched the sleeve of his shirt. "Pretty sharp."

"I'm the best-dressed homeless person in Manhattan!" His grin covered his face. "After all, I was voted the best-dressed student in my college!" He continued talking, but his reference to college lingered in my mind.

"People donate differently. That's what I call it, donate, cause I never ask for anything. People just see a need and fill it." He removed his sunglasses, breathed on them and wiped them on his shirt. His eyes met mine momentarily and they were clear and vibrant.

J.C. pulled a plastic bag out from behind him and had me peck in at the wrapped sandwiches. "Food people usually stay food people. Money people sometimes become clothes people, maybe seeing my gloves with holes in them, and then they bring me new gloves or new clothes in bags from department stores. People get

16

slighted if I don't wear the clothes they give me, so I always try to wear each sweater, shirt or pants I'm given, sometimes layering on more clothes than the weather demands. It's a funny thing about generosity; it makes people feel good to give but they feel better when they see the item being used. 'Where's that sweatshirt I gave you?' or 'How does that shirt fit?'and then I go on and on about how warm it is, or how it's the perfect size. They love these discussions. They like the feeling they get by helping someone in need."

I looked at his shirt, the one I had picked up for him earlier. He was right; I did feel good when I saw him wearing it. His perceptions were as clear as drops of rain on a windshield. He had a wise intuitiveness about him that didn't come from textbooks. And he showed such sophistication in his appreciation of others. So different from the many stories I had heard about the homeless.

"I get so much stuff -- metro passes, toiletries, stamps, and gift certificates. People are so generous! One man gave me a subway token once and I said, 'Thank you. This is the key to my house.' He seemed perplexed and then I added, 'The subway is my home.' He laughed a little nervously and moved on, probably surprised that I could joke about it."

"Is that where you sleep, J.C.? On the subway?"

"Yeah, cheapest room in the city!" He chuckled very easily and added, "In the park too, when the weather's decent."

I was learning a little more about J.C. today. I was fascinated by how he managed his homeless situation in such a business-like manner. His positive attitude was refreshing.

"Where do you keep all your things?" I noticed he didn't have many bags, unlike many of the shopping cart homeless I saw. "Do you carry everything around with you?"

He glanced around. "Oh, I keep my things here and there."

He started dismantling his cups and putting them in his backpack. He didn't want to answer me and I wasn't sure why. I watched him put the crates back under the phone booth and throw away the trash around him. It was as if he was cleaning house and if he had a broom, I'm sure he would have swept the sidewalk. He saw me watching him. "They like having me here," he said, "the management at Carnegie Hall. Better me than someone else. I guess they like having a well-mannered and famous homeless person sitting next to such a renowned institution." His grin covered his face like a Cheshire cat.

I laughed, amazed at his humor and also at his sense of purpose. He had found his home here.

> Earth's crammed with heaven.
> *Elizabeth Barrett Browning*

ß Safety First

On my way to see J.C. on Sunday, the streets were quiet except for nicely dressed families walking to church. "Probably going home to a Sunday dinner together or out to breakfast afterwards," J.C commented, his face looking drawn and tired. I was surprised to see him out here on Sunday morning. "I can't miss a Sunday, too many church people and tourists." Today he was wearing a red tie and his shirt collar was buttoned up tightly. Sunday clothes, I thought as I complimented him. "So where are you from, J.C.?"

"North Carolina. A town called New Bern. Sits right on the water, a nice seaport town, small but safe. Some famous sports people from there."

"Like who? "

"Well, Walt Bellamy played with the Knickerbockers, Bobby Perry with the San Francisco Giants, and Bobby Mann with the Greenbay Packers."

I didn't know much about sports so I couldn't show I was very impressed but he seemed to be very proud of these facts.

"What about you, Laurie. Where are you from?"

"Well, I'm from Cleveland but I live in Columbus, Ohio, now."

"Oh yes. I've been in Ohio. New York is a little different, don't you think?"

I laughed. "Yeah, slightly."

"Well, just be careful, Laurie. This city isn't like your small town." He regarded me somberly, his raised eyebrows reflecting concern. "Don't stop for any reason, especially to look at a map. People will know you're a tourist for sure."

I shook my head. "I know. I try to be careful."

"Diversion. That's what they do. If someone asks you for the time, just keep walking. While you're looking at your watch, they'll

19

be looking at your bag as they run down the street with it. I know. I've seen it all."

I grasped the strap of my bag as he talked. I had already taken many precautions since I came here--keeping my money in my pocket and leaving my credit cards at home. I had heard the stories, too. I told him so.

He didn't seem satisfied. "I saw you stop and talk to that homeless woman the other day, over by that doorway." He pointed toward the side door alcove along the building.

"Oh, you mean Glorious. Yeah, she didn't want the bagel I got for her. She kept saying no and I had just bought it for her. It was still warm and fresh." I had seen Glorious several times before sometimes on the street corner muttering and laughing to herself. When I stopped in front of her and said hello and asked her name, she met my eyes and the muttering stopped. I felt sorry for her.

"Don't do that," J.C. continued. "You could be handing her some food and she might grab your hair or scratch your face." His voice quieted slightly. "You have to be wary of homeless people."

"But you're homeless, J.C." My face had a hint of a smile.

He laughed, realizing what he had just said. "I'm the exception, though."

He is the exception, I thought, as I walked home. He worried about my safety like a parent who puts a child on the bus for the first time. Sometimes that's how I felt trying to find my way around New York.

I walked by his post one morning, and his cups were there but he wasn't. I walked several blocks to my bench in the park, and was surprised to see J.C. walking towards me from the opposite direction. He was holding a bag and drinking from it. It probably was just juice, but I wondered if it was liquor. As he approached, he pulled out a can of soda and my compassion kicked in.

"Are you okay?" I asked.

"Sure, just had to use the restroom is all." He pointed toward the playground. "They're over there, just in case you ever need to know." He paused for a moment. "I was afraid I would miss you.

20

Don't want to miss my main meal!" He looked at the bag I was holding.

"Well, I'm glad you're all right. Here you go. Enjoy!"

J.C. walked on and I watched him, noticing his thin shoulders and slow-paced walk. It felt different seeing him somewhere other than the corner and he seemed more homeless to me, more vulnerable in a way. There was no smell of alcohol, and I believed what he said, but I felt uncomfortable that he had been looking for me. It was just strange that he showed up at the place where I came every morning.

The next day he had a smug look on his face. "I thought I might find you there yesterday."

I looked at him. "What do you mean?" My gut started to knot up, that familiar feeling of fear starting to fester.

"I knew that's where you go every day. So when I had to go to the restroom, I thought I might run into you."

"But how . . ." I began.

"I was worried about you." His face was ladened with concern. "I had a friend of mine follow you one day and he told me where you sat. It's safe there, but just don't go any further into the park. Lots of things go on in Central Park. You have to be careful."

I didn't know if I should thank him or yell at him. After all, he said he was thinking about my safety, yet I was upset that he had someone follow me. "Don't worry. I always try to be safe." I wanted to say more but I decided to give him the benefit of the doubt. It bothered me as I thought about it later in the day. I decided to change my routine and try out different locations.

I saw him walking away from his corner around 12:30 p.m. and he caught a bus by Central Park. I wondered where he was going. Did he just ride the bus all day or did he have a destination? Was he meeting friends or did he have a girlfriend? And where did he keep all his things?

21

Every human being has the potential for compassion.
I have chosen to pay more attention to it.
Dalai Lama

4 An Ordinary Life

I found a sitting area across from Lincoln Center, a greenspace next to a high-rise apartment building. I sat on a bench that overlooked lavender and white blooms and water trickling over rocks. A thin-hair, bony-necked man sat next to a woman in a wheelchair, and he held her hand. The sun was a lacy veil over the buildings and the small trees.

I had a lot of writing to do. About my latest conversations with J.C. mostly but also about what I had been reading and why I had become so interested in this topic. I guess that's another reason why I decided to find a new place to sit; I purposely chose a place where I wouldn't be bothered.

I was spending less time talking to J.C. Although I was curious about his life and still felt like I wanted to help him somehow, I had some reservations since he said he had me followed. When he said one day that he needed a girlfriend, my antenna registered a possible flirtation that I wanted to avoid. Although the mere logistics of relationships would discourage intimacy among the homeless, homelessness was actually a subculture, and whenever people interacted, relationships formed. J.C. seemed to set his expectations high and would probably be very particular as to whom he spent time with. I didn't want him to think I was a viable option.

I was getting more courageous about exploring different parts of the city, though, and was becoming "street smart." I'd only turn down streets where other people were walking and wouldn't stop and open my wallet or bag while I was waiting at a crosswalk. Maybe I was being too cautious, but I remembered J.C.'s advice, "You can never be too careful." When I went back to Ohio for a few weeks, it was a relief that I didn't have to be as watchful as I was in

Manhattan.

I was hesitant to use the subway at first but realized that the subways from the seventies were now cleaned up. In the nineties, everyone used the subway. But there were always articles in the newspaper about robberies and assaults in Central Park and on the subways. In spite of these stories, the crime rate was supposedly down.[9] But I wasn't so sure, after reading about the homeless man who pushed a woman onto the subway tracks.

One cool September day, the wind moved between the buildings and created a tunnel effect while I talked with J.C. A man walked by and greeted him warmly. "I'm doing good," the man said. "Got a job now but I'm still short on cash. Can you spare a dollar?"

J.C. reached into his pocket and pulled out a dollar bill.

"Thanks, Bro." The young man gave him a high-five. "Now I can get me some lunch."

"That is a very good, very religious man," J.C. said to me later. "He donates to me, not much, but it's the thought that counts. He showed me where to trade in my change over at the A&P and I couldn't thank him enough for that. He's just real considerate."

He seemed to be in a reflective mood today. "You know, J.C. I've been thinking, I'd like to ask you some questions, but I don't want you to think I'm nosy."

"Not at all. I like talking to you. It's hard for me to have a decent conversation with anyone out here, so go ahead. Ask."

"But doesn't it hurt you to have me standing here? I mean, people don't seem to stop as much."

"Having you here improves my image, so to speak. And you know, sometimes conversation is a lot more important than donations." He waved his hand in a gesturing manner. "So, go ahead. Ask."

"Well, what did you do before this?" I hoped he'd tell me about being a teacher.

"Before panhandling? It's an art you know." He smiled a mischievous smile. "I'll tell you all about it sometime. But some other things first. Well, I mentioned I was a teacher, didn't I? Taught in North Carolina, Virginia, and here. You wouldn't know it by looking at me now, would you?"

I shrugged my shoulders, remembering his previous comment about a former student. "What did you teach?"

"I taught math and science. Junior high and high school." He laughed. "Under all this gray hair and ball cap is a very intelligent brain!" J.C. studied my face, maybe noticing I wasn't convinced. "I'll tell you about myself and you'll understand." He caught my eyes with a quick glance. "How old do you think I am?"

I looked at his thinning gray hair, tight curls against his neck and his bushy eyebrows flecked with white, in contrast to his smooth skin. I shook my head. "I don't know, J.C. Tell me."

"Sixty-seven. Born in 1931." He beamed at the surprise on my face. "Someone told me once that if I dyed my hair and beard, I could pass for thirty!" He pulled on his beard slightly, thinking for a moment. "But no, I am who I am. Now what else can I tell you?"

"I just wondered, I guess, if you had any family."

"Well, I have four brothers. Actually, I had four--three of them have passed. Went to church, bible school, prayer meetings, and revivals. You name it. My favorite passage--Isaiah 41:10--got me through some hard times as I got older."

"What is it?" I was curious about what kind of message inspired him.

"You probably don't realize it, but I'm a very religious person. I can't understand how someone can't believe in God. I mean, even if matter is formed from matter, there has to be a place where it all started. To me, that's where God comes in." I nodded, and started to say something, but he cut me off. "So look up that quote. You'll see what I mean. Anyway, my parents taught us the value of education and hard work early on--got us up at the crack of dawn to get water from the well before we left for our two-mile walk to school. My mother was a laundress; we'd come home for lunch and haul more water to the large buckets for her. If we were lucky, we'd catch a ride back to school on the back of someone's truck after they dropped off their laundry. I always worked, mowing lawns, shining shoes, and delivering groceries and newspapers. We took our studies seriously, mostly to avoid getting whipped. I did well in school. My

24

parents wanted me to be a doctor. They said the world was mine, anything was possible. I was a natural leader--I had a way of getting people to listen to me. My brothers said I got my way all the time, although they may have just been jealous of me." He beamed as he talked.

"You do have a way of being heard," I kidded. He smiled and continued.

"I grew up with segregation in the 1930's and 1940's. Schools, neighborhoods, buses, churches, and community activities were separate so there was always that message that we had to live apart from whites. I took in all the news and media, letting the lies about my race pass through me. I wouldn't let anything thwart me. I'd see humor in things that others didn't. I remember laughing when I was little and saw the signs, 'Colored Water' and 'White Water' at the drinking fountain, and somehow expected our water to be radiantly rich in color. Who wouldn't want 'colored water' when given the choice!"

I laughed as I thought about it. "Where did you go to college?"

"After I graduated from high school in 1951, I joined the Air Force. After two years, I decided to just stay in the Reserves and moved to Raleigh, North Carolina, and went to Shaw University on a football scholarship. I majored in math and science. I became a leader in my school--the first sophomore to ever become student body president." He sat up taller and his shoulders moved forward.

But he was moving too fast for me. "J.C. About your family. Were your brothers older than you were? Did they go to college? Were you close to them?"

He stopped talking and turned his head and looked at me with serious eyes. He moved his hand to silence me, his voice getting louder as he continued his story. He sure didn't like being interrupted. "I got to help choose speakers for the church vesper services; actually arranged for Martin Luther King, Jr. to come and speak. This was before he was famous, just a young preacher at a church in Alabama. I'll never forget the impact he made on me."

He paused and pulled on his beard as if he was remembering that time in his life.

"Anyway, in 1955 my mother passed away, and I dropped out of school. I took her death hard, but I kept my feelings bottled up inside. Eventually, my brother convinced me to get back in school. I jumped back in school full of vigor and was picked to be the student representative to the State Capital in Raleigh in my junior year. I received advanced placement credit for many courses. I was a go-getter--always looking for a challenge."

"I went to medical school at Colorado A & M, but grew tired of school. I dropped out, moved to Virginia and got my teaching certificate. Teaching suited me; the next year I was chairman of the Math Department. Bought a home and converted the front of the house into a restaurant, the Blue Star Restaurant and Soda Fountain. I decided to give up my teaching job and just run the restaurant."

I was having a hard time keeping up with his story. His life seemed normal--a close family with a strong work ethic and religious values. College-educated and teacher. But he never mentioned a wife. He had to have been married. I couldn't imagine him always being alone. "Did you ever marry or have kids?"

"Don't believe in marriage." His face met mine, and he started to say more but then just continued with his story.

"The restaurant business wasn't panning out, so I decided to look for another teaching job. But I wanted more adventure in my life, being used to having a lot of things going on. When my cousin asked me to go to New York City with him in the summer, I thought, 'Why not? New York City is supposed to be an exciting place to live. I'll look there.' So my cousin and I drove to New York, and I knew right away this was where I belonged." He added with a big grin. "You know, I actually got to try out for the New York Jets. This was in the early sixties. I was quite a star!"

"I taught in Long Island at two different schools during that time. After I became an Associate Principal and Chairman of the Math Department, I bought a house on Long Island. My job was going well so I bought another home through my G.I. loan, planning to rent it. But I got in over my head when I bought my third home. It seemed like a good investment at first, but the house needed so many repairs that the rental income couldn't keep up with the bills. I owed money to everyone. I knew that a teacher's salary was higher in the city, so I went back to Manhattan." He stopped abruptly. "Be sure you manage your money well. Don't get in over your head."

That's what he did, I thought. "Why didn't you just sell the houses, or at least the one that needed the repairs?"

He didn't answer but just shrugged his shoulders and continued talking. "I got an apartment in Manhattan. I taught at Joan of Arc Junior High, the Fashion Industry School, and then at Booker T. Washington Junior High School."

I continued to probe. "But why did you change schools so often, J.C?" I couldn't understand. I had been teaching for over ten years at the same school and most of the teachers I worked with didn't change schools unless there was a conflict with the principal, other teachers, or a need to make a grade level change. J.C. changed schools over and over again, but he always taught math at each school.

He stood up and stretched his legs and checked his watch. "It's getting late, Laurie."

I realized that he really didn't want to talk anymore and seemed irritated by my questions.

He said, "My record speaks for itself," when I probed him for proof. His story amazed me but I didn't know if it was true. It was like I was reading a novel, wanting to turn to the last page to see how the story ended. But I could see how it turned out--after all, here he was, homeless. It was those chapters in between that I needed to hear. And it bothered me that he didn't answer my questions. It was as if he already knew what he wanted me to know and he didn't want to address the details.

Later that week he told me more in bits and pieces.

"Well, the wear and tear of working with junior high and high school students was starting to affect me. I'd been teaching for about 15 years and was ready to do something else. I needed to make more money. I eventually landed a job as a medical examiner. I had some experience in the medical field from working as a xray technologist in the Air Force, and I had also been a correction officer. I was able to start paying off some of my debts."

"J.C., you've had so many different jobs. Couldn't you find a job now?"

He shrugged his shoulders. "The time just hasn't been right. Just hasn't been right."

Why, I wondered. I started to ask, but he changed the subject.

"Things were going well for me. But that soon changed. A car accident--and I hurt my back real bad. I couldn't drive and was forced to go on disability. My rent was too high so I got a cheaper place, city housing. It was pretty decent, stained glass windows, hardwood floors, and arched doorways. I earned extra money by doing private tutoring. I lived comfortably, but I ate at soup kitchens and got clothing from my church cause of my low funds."

J.C. stopped and took a deep breath. "So now you have it."

"Well, what happened? I mean, how did you end up here?"

J.C. put his cups down for a minute, took off his glasses and rubbed his eyes. "Well, there's more to the story, a lot more. It's going to have to wait til tomorrow."

I didn't want to wait, but he'd been talking for more than an hour. "You sure, J.C.? I have the time."

"No. I'll keep you in suspense. It's better this way. I know that you'll be back just to hear more," he teased.

"Well, thanks. You shared a lot." I gave him a smile. "You know, I'm sorry if I kept interrupting you. It's just that I want to understand everything you're telling me."

"I know, but try not to interrupt my flow of thought, okay? Save your questions for later."

"Okay." I realized that when he was focused on one thing, he didn't want to be sidetracked. "So, I'll see you tomorrow? Same time?"

I was glad we decided to call it a day. I was exhausted, trying to follow J.C.'s story of his life, trying to make sense of how the years moved at such a fast pace in his recollection. He talked so casually, so matter of factly, and watching him talk about his life's accomplishments as he sat on the corner panhandling was an image hard to find credible. I had no reason not to believe him, and I had no reason to believe him. But I was very fascinated. If his story was just

28

fabrication, then he was a talented storyteller. If it was true, then how could he have ended up here on this street corner?

The next day he talked more about his family, and he said he hadn't been in contact with any of them since his father died in 1969. The whole idea of isolation--no friends to speak of and estrangement from family--characteristics typical of the homeless. J.C. talked about his brother, Tom, at length, mentioning how he always looked out for him when he was a kid.

"He was the second oldest and somehow saw to it that I learned what I needed to know," said J.C., looking at me again with reflective eyes. "He taught me how to ride a bike, play chess, drive a car, play football, and how to draw. He worked at J.C. Penney and made sure I was the best dressed guy at my high school." J.C. laughed. "He knew how much I loved looking good, even back then!" He slowed down his speech and added, "I probably miss him the most. He was my brother, but he was also my friend." He closed his eyes for a second. "I wonder if he is still alive? He'd be in his seventies now, I guess, since he's older than me."

"And my other brothers? Well, Lewis had a drinking problem and that's probably what he died from. It's because of him that I never got involved with alcohol. Now my brother, William Earl, is the one who said I needed to get myself back to college when I dropped out. He was in the Air Force, too, studying to be a lawyer but also ended up teaching. I know that he passed away. Must have been back in the sixties or thereabouts."

When J.C. talked about his family, I felt like maybe he wished he hadn't broken ties with them, but when I asked him about it, he said that after going back to North Carolina for his father's funeral, he knew he never wanted to go back there again.

"Why not?"

"I didn't fit in there. It wasn't that I had hard feelings for any of them, it was just that this was a different time in my life and I was ready to move on to something else."

My thoughts kept me awake that night. J.C.'s words kept jumping into my consciousness each time I started to doze off, jerking me awake as if I just touched a hot iron. There just had to be a reason he didn't keep in touch with his family in North Carolina.

I wanted to verify his educational and teaching background. It turned out it wasn't too difficult to do and I actually found several news articles: one from New Bern when he graduated from high school and another when he graduated from college. My biggest surprise was locating a 1963 high school yearbook from Wyandanch High School with his picture in it. He looked so different that I wouldn't have known it was him if his name wasn't there.

He could have been a colleague of mine, I thought, any of the teachers I had worked with over the years. Why him and not them? I knew I was talking to a very intelligent person and now everything he told me explained why. I had to hear the rest of the story—what happened to him?

> God will find a mouth to tell you what you need to know.
>
> *Unknown*

5 The Nightmare

"You spend a lot of time talking to him, Laurie," my husband commented one morning as I got ready to leave. "What do you think really happened to him?"

I had been sharing all along the details of J.C.'s story with my husband. He was also intrigued but more skeptical than I was. He kept saying, "Don't do anything stupid" and I assured him I was being careful. He hadn't talked to J.C. like I did each day. He only knew what he heard from me.

I didn't know why I was so taken in by J.C. Part of me was so curious about his situation and part of me was taken in by his charm. I was basically a shy person but because of my interest in the homeless and J.C.'s pleasant demeanor, it was easy to just keep talking to him. He sat so regularly on his corner and others reacted favorably to him too. There were many others who talked to him for awhile each day, and he mentioned Nina and Donald in particular. "They knew me from the beginning. Started donating to me right away on a regular basis. I don't know what I would have done without them," he commented one morning. I hadn't met them yet but was anxious to find out what they knew about him.

"Good morning, Lady Laurie. You're looking lovely on this picture perfect day." J.C. always had a compliment for me. I gave J.C. a bag with an egg sandwich from the deli. I shifted my weight as I half-listened to his words of thanks. I wanted to continue our conversation from the other day.

J.C. seemed to read my mind. "You've been thinking about me and wondering a lot of things, haven't you?" His dark sunglasses covered his eyes, but I could see a hint of a sparkle. "Well, I want to tell you how I ended up here."

"I started panhandling by accident. I didn't know it was called that back then. I'd given change to homeless people on the streets without a moment's thought. I stood outside of Mickey Mantle's, a local restaurant here, thinking about what to do next. I just finished some coffee and a man walked by and put a dollar in my empty cup. I took it out and nervously said, 'Thank you.' I hadn't been asking for money, yet it seemed right to say something. Then someone else put money in my cup. I thought, this cup must be magical cause this isn't natural. It was embarrassing, yet I was hungry and I needed this money. But I moved on and walked around the corner. I don't know what led me to Seventh Avenue and 57th Street, but I stood there with my cup and more people dropped money into it. Another homeless man stood nearby, singing softly while his head swayed slowly. He jiggled the coins in his cup. 'You can't stand here.' His dark eyes weighed heavily on my face. 'This is my corner. Go across the street.' He wasn't rude to me, just telling me the first rule of panhandling: Don't intrude on someone else's turf."

I stood up to get J.C.'s attention. "I mean, not just how you ended up here on this corner." My voice quieted slightly. "How did you become homeless in the first place?"

"Oh, that's what everyone wants to know." He adjusted his sunglasses and leaned forward. "You see, I had some real bad luck. I never thought I'd end up here, though." He stopped suddenly and looked around, his head moving back and forth like a wind-up toy. His voice quieted. "I hate talking here. Too many nosy people." He motioned to the vendors across from him. "They watch me all the time, trying to read my lips. They're no good, just no good, I tell you."

I was taken aback by his changed demeanor, his face nervous and eyes cold as steel. I didn't know what to say. "Well, we can go somewhere else and talk," but as I said those words I thought, where? Where can I go with a homeless person?

"Yeah, some place else." J.C.'s shoulders moved up and down quickly. "Let me think. Let me think." He smoothed his shirt, squeezed his hands together and sighed heavily.

I was beginning to feel like maybe this was a mistake. J.C. clearly had some issues, and the way he was acting concerned me. Yet, I really wanted to ask him some questions. "How about that coffee shop across the street? I'll buy you breakfast," I suggested.

J.C. stood up suddenly. "I got it. McDonald's. I know exactly where we can sit." He started getting his things together and we headed down the street. He politely positioned himself on my right I noticed, but I felt a little conspicuous walking with him. The familiar adage, "appearances always matter" surfaced to my consciousness, but I didn't care what people thought. I didn't know anyone here anyway. I wanted to help him carry his things, but I just walked beside him and he told me how he frequently went to McDonald's to use the restroom. He knew the manager there so no one hassled him for using the facilities without making a purchase.

We reached the corner of 56th and Eighth Avenue. I started to push open the side door. "No, not that door." J.C. took my arm and moved me alongside him to the front door. What am I doing, I thought, realizing his need to be in charge. But this is a safe place, and I really want to talk to him, I told myself as J.C. guided me inside.

"Wait, wait a minute," he said quietly. "This isn't good. Isn't good." His words were spoken with precision. He looked around the room and then said, "Over there," and I followed him to an empty table. "I usually sit by that window. I can see who's outside that way."

I looked over and saw a woman and young child sitting in a booth. I took this all in, how carefully J.C. picked a place to sit; he looked around always checking things out, as if he were expecting something to happen. Who was he looking for? He was so watchful and vigilant. Has probably had some bad experiences, I thought. Maybe living on the streets for so long had made him paranoid about others.

I was seeing a different side of J.C. today. His overconcern about others watching him and listening to him both at his corner and at McDonald's; his need to be in control. This wasn't the relaxed, easygoing J.C. I knew.

"But this table is okay. It's okay." We sat down, and again I felt like everyone was watching us. I looked at J.C., and his face began to relax and I saw him not as a homeless person, but as a person who just happened to be homeless. He nodded and looked at me. "So Miss Laurie, now I can tell you my story."

"I lived in Harlem--a fairly nice apartment for the area. But things started changing--lots of movement going on, in and out of my building all hours of the night. Loud voices, doors opening and closing, people not making eye contact. Drugs were being dealt out with the efficiency of shuffling a deck of cards. People moved out, neighbors who had been there for years. New people moved in, young people dressed in fancy clothes. You should have seen them. Leather jackets, slicked-back hair, and high, black-polished boots. It was hard to ignore what was happening, so I just took it all in."

Drugs. So that was it. He was involved in drugs. He didn't seem like he was anymore; at least he always seemed coherent and alert. Couldn't be using drugs now.

"I should have taken my belongings and found another place to live. But I was stubborn. This was my home; I had fixed it up, and I didn't want to leave. But they found out about my apartment and that was it."

"What do you mean, J.C.?"

"Well, the other apartments were a mess. Trash was piled up outside doors and old furniture sat on the curb. My apartment was like a palace in the midst of a slum, an ideal place for the drug dealers to carry on their dealings. A perfect spot to wine and dine and seal off deals. The problems started when the superintendent of the building stopped by to fix my heat. He looked my apartment over, his face shifting slowly from disinterest to delight. I overheard him in the hallway later. 'Hey, have you seen J.C.'s apartment? It's the best in this building."

"So you knew what they were up to?"

"I assumed they wanted my apartment. That's how drug dealers operate. They need a base to work from, and they like fine things. Anyway, three men I didn't know stood in the hallway, demanding to come inside. I cracked the door slightly and kept the chain on, but

34

they broke it open. They moved past me and scoped the place. I stood back and watched them make themselves comfortable. The air was fresh and clean. The refrigerator was full. They walked carefully on the polished wood floor, but they dropped their ashes on the rug. One huge man walked toward the couch and sat down, kicked off his shoes, and closed his eyes. He had a puzzled look on his face when he surveyed the room. They wanted my apartment. I pleaded with them, said I had been here a long time, couldn't they find another place? But no, they wanted my place. They said they'd do their business here at night while I slept. I had to keep the door unlocked at all times. When they left, I collapsed, and my heart was pounding in fear."

"J.C., I don't understand. These people were just going to move into your apartment? Couldn't you complain to your landlord?"

"Laurie, things are different in Harlem. And you don't mess with drug dealers. Ever. So anyway, they returned like they said they would. Their loud voices and endless laughter kept me up at night. And there was always something they wanted or needed. I hardly ever slept. They knew what they were doing--they wanted me to be uncomfortable. Sometimes my door would open to blaring music and they'd laugh, saying, 'Hey, J.C. Come out and join the fun!' Each morning I cleaned up the mess in the living room; the water marks left on the tables, the ashes on the floor, food on the rug, the kitchen sink stained with colored liquids and white powder, broken bottles, empty cans, and trash everywhere."

"Were there many of them, J.C?"

"Oh yeah. It always started out slow, but then I bet there were at least 15 or 20 people out there. Then they started coming earlier, and in the morning they'd be sprawled out on the living room floor. Pretty soon the only privacy I got was to just leave my apartment. One night when I got back, the apartment was empty so I locked the door. But at two o'clock in the morning, they broke it open. And I paid, really paid. They beat me up, and I barely slept that night. I wondered what I was going to do."

"You should have just left, J.C. It sounds like it only kept getting worse."

"It's not that simple. I knew too much now--I knew their faces, I knew what went on every night. I think they were ready to get rid of me, though, by the way they kept bothering me. When they changed the lock one night when I was out, I knew I couldn't take it any longer. I had to leave. I had to get out of there. I looked at my furniture, my music collection, my clothing, my pictures, and my books. What should I take, I thought, or rather, what will they let me take?"

"Somehow they read my mind. They wanted my apartment and they wanted it as it was. They didn't want me to disturb its contents by removing things they had learned to depend upon."

J.C.'s gaze on me felt like a magnet drawing me in. I started to ask another question but he put up his hand as if to silence me.

"The door burst open, mid-afternoon. Two tall men I hadn't seen before pushed me out of their way. They forced me to leave with only a small bag of my belongings."

"They forced you?"

"They pushed me out the door, beat me up, tore my clothes. And they had guns." J.C. paused for a moment. "They took everything that was mine. I hoped they wouldn't find my money hidden in the walls. The only other money I had was a few hundred dollars that I kept at a friend's house. I was so weak and in so much pain and barely made it to my friend's place."

"You didn't go to the police?"

"I couldn't. I'd seen the comings and goings of my apartment building and there was nothing going on there that the police didn't already know about. I'd been following the stories in the newspaper about officers overlooking drug dealing in exchange for money and drugs, some acting as guardians for dealers by protecting the buildings and stores where they lived and worked. I didn't know if this was happening where I lived, but I was afraid to go to the police.[10] I feared for my life, that was for sure. I couldn't tell anyone. I wouldn't tell anyone. I knew enough about the drug business to know that noone likes a squealer. No matter how much I lost or how much I hurt, I knew I had to go on. I stopped at a coffee shop to use the restroom and wash up. I finally took a seat at a corner table while the waitress stared at me. I sipped hot coffee and contemplated my next step. I had no plan. I was robbed of all my belongings and my self-worth. I stayed with my friend those first few nights until I got my strength back. I got my money from him and then left. I didn't want to impose."

J.C. stopped talking. In a solitary moment, his shoulders relaxed, his breathing slowed and he met my eyes and probably noticed the turn of my shoulders toward him, letting him know that he had my undivided attention. I wanted to ask him some questions, but I could see the exhausted look in his eyes. I gave him a half-smile. "Let's go, okay?"

We left McDonald's and walked down the street. I felt closer to him somehow, just knowing more about his life. I grasped his hand as I turned the corner to head home. I squeezed it for a moment, wanting to say something. "It hasn't been easy for you, has it?"

He just shook his head and shrugged his shoulders. "You're a good listener, Miss Laurie. I'll see you tomorrow."

> Responsibility is just a formalized way of caring
> and once we let go of doing only what's appropriate,
> we can then embrace the essence of our knowing souls.
> *Laurie Anthony*

6 Remembering Back

My feet moved like bricks and I walked to the park instead of going straight home. My thoughts rested heavy as if they were tired from being on a long journey. I wanted to open my mind like a suitcase and remove each thought with deliberate care. I needed time to digest everything J.C. had told me and make sense of it

I didn't know what to think. Could something like this really happen? Were drug dealers really lurking between buildings and were drugs circulating the streets? Did they terrorize people like this? Were policemen really on the take? I knew I was naïve about a lot of things, but I had grown up and lived only in the suburbs of Ohio. No matter what I had read, or how many times I had watched N.Y.P.D. Blue on television, I still couldn't grasp the reality of what J.C. was telling me. Why did he keep living in a building if he knew what was happening there? Did he think he could come and go as he pleased in a building that housed drug dealers? Was he more involved than he let on? A nagging voice inside me questioned, "Is this real? Did this really happen?"

But J.C. spoke with such passion and conviction as if he were reliving every moment of it. I wondered where he went after he left his friend's apartment. An emergency shelter? A social service agency? Or did he just resign himself to living on the streets?

I knew there had to be more to all of this. I was intrigued by J.C.'s story. He was college educated, an Air Force veteran, a teacher, and then became homeless because of drug criminals. He had a story to tell and I wondered if I could help him tell it.

Many leaves dropped from the trees as the mornings took on

frigid temperature. The morning crowd seemed to move along the sidewalk at a brisker pace than normal and policemen planted their feet at the busy intersection. I slowed down when I saw J.C. bundled up in his heavy gray jacket over several sweaters.

"Hi, J.C." I smiled. "You know, I can always gauge the temperature outside by counting your layers of clothing."

"Gotta keep warm, you know, and this sure helps." He pointed to the scarf and hat I brought him last week. "I don't know what I'd do without you, L.A."

"Oh, you have lots of friends, J.C." I flashed him a smile.

"No one like you. I think you must read my mind sometimes." He held out his feet clad in his new tennis shoes. "You think of everything." I had picked those up for him when I was back in Ohio over the holidays for a good price. "Hey," he continued. "I enjoyed our talk yesterday, Lady Laurie. Hope I didn't get carried away talking too much."

"Not at all. In fact, I just kept thinking about everything, over and over again last night. You know what I think. Someone should write a book about you."

"You know, I've had my share of offers. When I tell people about my background, they get real curious. I think I must be the most well-known homeless person here in Manhattan!"

"Why haven't you had anyone write it? You could make lots of money."

"Maybe I will. But I don't trust anyone to get it right. I probably should just write it myself."

"I'd love to write your story, J.C. I'd do a good job." I told him this might be a way to make him some money and he seemed interested.

He looked at me for a few moments, his eyes not leaving my eyes, somehow reaching deep inside them searching for something. He looked up with a complacent smile on his face. "You may be the one to write my story, Miss L.A. You just might be the one. Something to think about, that's for sure."

"Well, I went to the library already, J.C.. I found some newspaper articles from the New York Times about drugs and police corruption."

"You did?" He gave me an inscrutable look.

"Yeah, and I made copies of some of the articles. There was a lot going on during the time you lost your apartment."

"I told you. I told you that was the case." His mouth formed into an easy smile. "I'm impressed, Laurie. You're quite the investigator. You're taking this very seriously."

"Well, think about this book idea, J.C., okay?"

The next day the gray morning sky was layered like shale, so different from the mesh sky lining the day before. When I saw J.C. he said, "Let's do it, Lady Laurie. Let's write a book."

I shook his hand and smiled. "It's a deal, then. But if we're going to do this, I want to interview you, J.C., and it's going to take some time. We have to have a place to talk without interruptions."

"You're right. Can't talk here." He looked at the vendors. "Did I ever tell you about what they did? How they went through my bags once when I left to use the restroom? Stole money from me, too! Couldn't believe it. Just couldn't believe it!" He looked around cautiously and then behind him. "Sometimes I think there are bugs in these walls too. It can be done, you know, I've seen it."

He was getting sidetracked and I brought him back. "Well, let's go over to that coffee shop and talk. I'll buy you lunch, okay." I looked at my watch. "How soon will you be done here?"

He thought for a moment. "No, I got things to do today. Maybe tomorrow. Let me think about it."

Things to do today, I wondered. Like what? I couldn't understand what a homeless person did all day. Did he structure his day like the rest of us? What does one do with large blocks of time that aren't broken up by grocery shopping, paying bills and driving kids around? Well, this will come up later, I thought, when I ask him some questions.

"You know, I do need time to get some questions together. Tomorrow is Thanksgiving, so let's shoot for Friday. Okay?"

It was pouring rain, the kind that seems to fall from every inch of the sky without every letting up. My husband and I waved at J.C. on our way to the parade. Couldn't miss the Macy's Day Parade, no matter what the weather, I thought. I decided that J.C probably would get a lot of good food on Thanksgiving, knowing how people looked after him. Many churches served meals, also.

After several hours of standing in the downpour, we gave in to the weather and headed home, our clothes soaked. J.C. was still sitting there, so we stopped and gave him a few dollars. "I'll have some leftovers for you tomorrow, J.C.," I said, wringing out the ends of my scarf.

I had struggled with a list of questions to ask J.C. Because of his evasiveness, I decided to just let him continue where he left off with his story. I was excited the next morning as I walked over to his corner, but not for long.

"Why not?" I asked dumbfoundedly after he said that today wasn't a good day.

"I was thinking. We need a tape recorder. You can't write fast enough to keep up with me. Yeah, a small tape recorder would work."

Next day . . . "I got a tape recorder, J.C."

"That's perfect," he said, holding it in his hand. Small and light." He paused for a moment. "But I need a microphone. I don't want to have to hold this up to my mouth all the time."

Next day . . . "I got a microphone, J.C."

"Great. Oh, but I'm not prepared today. I have to travel lighter if we're going to go to a restaurant."

I was getting discouraged and a little irritated. Everything had to be just the way he wanted; he always had to be in charge. Maybe he was having second thoughts about the book. "You know, J.C., maybe you could just start writing down some things for now and then we can start the interviewing later."

"No, I speak better than I write. If I were writing, I'd be so worried about grammar and spelling that I would use easy words and never get my point across. No, interviewing is the best. But I was thinking, the coffee shop might be too busy. People in and out, listening to what we're saying and then we'd feel like we could only sit there for so long without ordering more food. No, I found a better spot. There's a bench over at the playground." He motioned toward the park. "The bench is by itself. No interruptions and no one to bother us." He looked pleased as he finished talking.

I was glad that we finally worked this out. This whole time he had been putting me off not because he didn't want to talk, but because he had to find a suitable location. I should have known, recalling when we went to McDonald's and how careful J.C. had been there. "The playground it is then. Tomorrow, say, at 12:00 p.m. I'll meet you there, okay?"

I can't explain what happened to me after that moment. I started

 getting somewhat nervous. A coffee shop was one thing, but the park? I walked over to the playground and felt better noticing many parents with their children. As long as there were other people there, I'd be fine, I told myself. But that night, I tossed and turned, and knots in my stomach kept me awake.

Familiar knots that signaled to me that deep inside something was wrong. Why am I so nervous about this, I wondered? It's about trust, mostly trusting myself to set boundaries, to be cognizant of what's happening and not let my naiveness direct my decisions. It was hard for me to trust him, though, because he lived in such a different world than me, not just now but before. It was as if this was just too big for me to take on, yet the compassion inside me was still strong.

The next morning I packed up my things, put fresh batteries and a tape in my recorder and walked to the playground. J.C. was already sitting on the bench, relaxed and enjoying the sunshine on his face, though the air was cold. One wouldn't know he was homeless if it weren't for the stuffed bags under the bench.

"Hi, J.C." I got my notes out. "Are you ready to begin?"

"Well, I'm a little nervous, but let's get started. Let me see that." I handed him the tape recorder. "Okay, now you got a new tape?"

I nodded.

"How about the batteries?"

"Brand new."

"Okay. I'm ready." He pushed the buttons. "Go ahead. Ask me a question."

"J.C. could you just continue where you left off? You said you had just left your friend's apartment. Where did you go after that?"

"The park. Central Park. I walked and walked for hours, resting on a bench once in awhile. I felt violated, losing everything, especially my self-respect. People sipped their coffee, adjusted their cameras, flipped through newspapers and walked by hand in hand. I didn't talk to anyone or meet anyone's eyes. I had to think, I had to think. They wanted my money, they wanted me. I knew too much and as long as I was out walking around, I was a risk to them. That night I fell asleep on a bench in Riverside Park next to another homeless person. I was afraid to fall asleep, fearful of being found."

J.C. turned off the tape recorder and rewound it. He played it back and listened. "Just wanted to make sure it's working. Now, I'm not going to go over again how I started panhandling. You remember that, Mickey Mantles's, blah-blah-blah."

"Yeah, I remember. Just start when you were on the corner panhandling, the first time."

He pulled on his beard for a moment and then began talking. "I went across the street and stood there all day, collecting coins, never asking for money, politely nodding as people gave me some change. I was quiet but pleasant and appreciative. I was hungry and thirsty, and when I counted my money, I had almost ten dollars, enough to go to the coffee shop across the street. I was treated very rudely there--I guess because of my appearance. I left storming mad without

43

even eating. I felt numb as I got on the bus to go home, forgetting for a moment that I didn't have one anymore. I looked in my backpack, taking a quick inventory of my belongings--a tee-shirt, my wallet, three napkins, one newspaper, my birth certificate, photos of my family, a few newspaper articles, one cup, a pair of jeans, socks, underwear, my driver's license, my social security card and Veteran's card. I realized how little I had left."

"Couldn't you sneak back into your apartment and get some of your things?"

"No, I didn't want to chance running into them. Even when the bus passed by my neighborhood, I was afraid they'd see me. All I could think of was that I needed to get some sleep. I got off at West 155th Street and started walking toward a quiet street, finding myself at a school playground. I sat on a swing and rocked back and forth. I was exhausted and tears covered my face. Slowing down, I noticed a bench under some trees in a field behind the school and went there. It was a cool fall evening, and I didn't have any blankets to make a bed so I layered my tee shirts and put my pack under my head. Some school kids saw me in the morning and they ran away screaming. I bolted upright and saw their heads turning to stare at me. I was now the person that teachers and parents warned kids about--the elusive 'stranger.' I grabbed my belongings and took off. 'I'm a teacher,' I thought, realizing now I was just a homeless person."

I couldn't imagine what that must have been like for him. He was right about how teachers and parents are always warning kids about strangers, and for good reason. Yet, it seemed so unfair to J.C.

"I stopped at a fast-food restaurant and used the restroom and looked in the mirror. No wonder I scared them, I thought, as I looked at my dusty face and matted hair. I threw some cold water on my face, washed my hands and started walking again. I wanted to stay in a hotel for a night to clean up and get my bearings. I hated to part with my money, but I needed to shower. I stopped at a drugstore and bought some toiletries. I stayed in the hotel room all day, only leaving to get some fast food. The hotel didn't have a television or phone but it had hot water and a warm bed. I curled up in a ball under the covers that night and slept hard."

"Didn't you know anyone that could help you, J.C.?" I raised my voice against the children playing. J.C. had lived here for so long I was sure he had to have people he could depend on. "Other friends?"

"No, people don't want to be bothered and I didn't want to impose on anyone. Besides, it was too risky."

No friends? I was surprised. He really must have isolated himself all these years. "Did you go to any agencies to get help?" I had made a few phone calls and found out the Coalition for the Homeless had several programs for homeless clients, including emergency and rental assistance.[11]

"No, I hadn't even gotten that far. I was still in shock over what had happened. And later, it was a matter of pride. I didn't want to use the government's money, other people's money."

Yet, what he was doing--panhandling--wasn't he still living off the money of others?

"I felt good as I left the hotel, wondering when I would sleep on a bed again. I stood outside a deli for awhile, hoping to catch people with change still in their hands. Then I moved in front of a bank, but people seemed less receptive there. I decided to return to the stairs of the subway station where it was busy and had been lucrative for me the day before. I stood at the corner of 57th and Seventh Avenue. My cup was still pretty empty so I still didn't stop panhandling. I tried to be pleasant, but most people just ignored me. One guy who had just gotten robbed, yelled at me about it because the man who robbed him was homeless. Even kids would mock me, assuming I was going to buy drugs or liquor with the money they put in my cup, just because I was homeless."[12]

"Eventually I could predict who would come by, depending on the time of day. People were starting to know me there, so this became the base I operated from. People dropped coins in my cup, and the minutes they spent talking to me made time move by quickly."

"So panhandling was getting you enough money for food?"

"Yeah, on good days. But it was hard sitting there hour after hour. My body was sore from sleeping on a bench."

I was curious about where he slept. "Do homeless people have their own turf when it comes to sleeping arrangements, also?"

"Yeah, some benches are already spoken for. So I had to do some homework on my own. Who would think choosing a park bench would be so difficult? I wanted privacy, so I picked a bench off the beaten path in an area where no one else slept. Next, I didn't want to be under any trees or in areas where bird droppings could land on me. Because of the street sweeps taking place in the city, I wanted a place secluded enough so I wouldn't be hassled by the police.[13] I tried several benches and slept pretty good and eventually got more blankets from a church to cushion my body."

J.C. talked on and on while I tried to envision his life as he explained it to me. He seemed comfortable talking, stopping only periodically to regroup his thoughts. He talked in a very organized and thorough way. I didn't have to make that effort to follow his train of thought like I did on his corner when he was busy greeting others. I felt like we were two friends just talking, and I could tell he enjoyed telling his story. He cracked jokes and laughed and kidded me about being so persistent. My heart went out to him. There was something childlike about him, although I knew his experiences were far from that.

I wondered if he talked to other homeless people. Did he buy his food from vendors or go into grocery stores or delis? Where did he clean up and change clothes?

He told me that he hung around Columbus Circle and talked to other homeless people to find out where to get food and clothing. The outreach vans for the homeless passed out food and toiletries every day at various locations. He got a "street sheet" from a Project Outreach volunteer that listed the addresses of soup kitchens, shelters, and food pantries including times and locations of meals.[14] He said that he pretty much just used the fountain, the restroom in the park, and fast-food restaurants for their facilities.

"Of course, I can't forget Al!"

"Who's Al?"

"Well, it's because of Al that I was able to stay clean--he'd let me use the restroom in the subway to clean up, and he always looked

46

out for me. Don't know what I would have done without him."

"Why didn't you try a shelter, J.C?" I didn't know much about shelters, but that's where I thought the homeless always went.

"I did, kind of. I'll tell you about it later on. Most nights I just walked around, unable to sleep for fear of being robbed or hurt. Homeless people slept in doorways or were stretched out on sidewalks. I avoided looking at their eyes--I could recognize other homeless people by their slow walk, their slumped shoulders, their heads hanging down. These were the homeless people I had never wanted to encounter, those who urinated on themselves and smelled of it, drunk and passed out on the sidewalk. I didn't fit the stereotype of a homeless person; at least that's what I thought. I still had the drive and the courage to change my situation."

"How were you going to do this?" I wasn't real impressed with his plan so far. Panhandling and sleeping in the park didn't seem like a very lucrative way to get off the streets.

J.C. looked at me curiously, and just said, "Don't worry. I'll get to that later. Now I depended only on the panhandling, and I got just barely enough for food and toiletries. I'd been wearing the same clothes for about six days now, and I dug through my bag trying to find something that didn't smell. I didn't have money for the laundromat so ended up washing my dirty clothes in the sink at the restroom, and laid them to dry on a bench. Sometimes I'd have to throw everything out and just start over, going back to the church to get more clothes. I tried to shower and clean up every couple days, but a place to stay cost fifty dollars a night."

"Was it an S.R.O.?" I had recently read about the "single room occupancy" rooms that had once been available to the homeless before the major hotels came in and demolished them.[15]

He set the microphone down. He looked at me, raised his eyebrows and gave me a half-smile. "I don't mean to be so abrupt with you, but your questions interrupt my train of thought. I'll tell you more later about where I stayed."

"Well, I'll just start raising my hand if I have a question, okay? Just like in school!" I kidded him about being so inflexible, and he laughed.

"I felt alone and afraid, but my need to survive was strong. Everything I felt or did went back to this instinct of survival--the food I ate, where I slept, sat or stood, who I talked to, how I carried my belongings, how I got money, and how I kept safe. All I thought about was what I needed to survive. But soon I was out of money."

"Why didn't you look for a job, J.C.?"

"I was in no position to look for a job. I was a mess, and no one would hire me in the state I was in." He spoke abruptly, as if I didn't know what I was even asking. "I had three things working against me--my age, my color and being homeless. You have to look presentable before someone will hire you. And you can't do that without a place to live."

I was beginning to feel his irritation. Maybe he had talked enough for one day. "Gosh, J.C. We've been sitting here for several hours already. Why don't we stop for today?"

He wiped his nose with a napkin and then nodded. "Whew. That's hard work. Remembering back, but once I started, it all came back to me, crystal clear."

"Why don't you take a few days off, J.C. This weather's gotta be bad for your cold."

"Yeah, maybe I will." He put the money in his zippered pocket and started getting his things together. "I enjoyed that, Miss L.A. I like talking to you. I just can't figure out where you came from! Did some angel send you or something!" He shook his head while looking at me very intently, with a slight grin. "One thing is for sure. You go out of your way to help me."

"I just do what I can, J.C." I wasn't sure why I was so compelled to help him. I was learning a lot in the process, and would probably never again be in a position to experience a friendship like this. J.C.'s charm was definitely captivating--I was experiencing a whole different world through his eyes.

I went home and took notes as I replayed the tape. I made a timeline of J.C.'s life, beginning with his childhood up to where he left off. I wasn't clear about the span of time from 1975 to 1992. Even though he mentioned a few things, it just seemed like such a long period of time to not have more to say. I wanted to pursue further why he didn't go to another social service agency to get help or Veteran's Administration, since he served in the Air Force. I was also confused about the "$50 a night" rooms he stayed in, but he hadn't explained that yet. I wrote down some of my observations-- his fastidiousness when choosing a bench to sleep on, his overconcern with the tape recorder, his annoyance with me when I interrupted him.

We set up another time to get together and talk. I needed a few days to process everything he told me, and I also wanted to spend some time at the library.

I found some news articles that dealt with the homeless in New York City and copied articles specifically about the subways, shelters, and panhandling. I checked out some books but relied on the internet for current statistics. I found some data on the homeless population from the 1998 U.S. Conference of Mayors' Report. [16]

Ethnicity		Gender	
Afro-American	49%	Single Male	45%
Caucasian	32%	Single Female	14%
Hispanic	12%	Families with children	38%
Asian	3%	Unaccompanied minors	3%
Native Americans	4%		

I was surprised by the statistics in a way. Most of the homeless people I saw in the midtown area were male and Afro-American. Yet, the statistics said that 32% of the homeless were Caucasian. Maybe the street homeless were predominantly black. The high percentage of families with children (over 1/3 of the homeless population) really disturbed me. Had it always been this way or was family homelessness on the rise?[17] And if so, why?

The situation for the homeless seemed pretty grim. I was determined to find out what programs had shown success in working with this population. So far, all I was finding was negative information. So I spent hour after hour, reading and searching on the internet and found a lot of information through several sites: National Coalition for the Homeless, the Department of Health and Human Services, National Resource Center on Homelessness and Mental Illness, and the National Law Center on Homelessness and Poverty. Along with this, I talked with various individuals who worked with the homeless. I was beginning to get a rounder picture of the homeless situation.[18] But even with the progress that was being made, there were still so many gaps in services.[19]

I saw Glorious again as I was walking around, and she recognized me and called out, "Hey, Mama." I stopped and smiled at her and asked, "Why did you call me Mama? I'm not that much older than you." She smiled slightly and said quietly, "It's just that everyone needs a mama." I walked away feeling saddened, wondering what her life must have been like. All the research on causes and solutions to homelessness didn't address the pain of that experience itself. Not just lacking the material comforts that one takes for granted every day, but the feeling that no one really cares. I wondered what the suicide rate was among the homeless.

I decided to pay J.C. for his interview time so our book project would seem like a business agreement. Before our next interview, I'd talk to him about it.

A smile costs nothing, but its value is priceless.
It enriches the one who gives it, yet does not impoverish him.

Anonymous

7 Holiday Cheer

The trees had all lost their leaves, and the winter snow had snuck up quietly. The December chill filled the air, and the streets glimmered with holiday lights.

"Hi, J.C." A blond-haired woman walked up and smiled a beautiful smile. I was standing next to J.C., and he introduced me to her. "Laurie, this is Nina."

"So, how are you today, J.C.?" Nina had on an angora pale rose hat that highlighted her cheeks. J.C. had mentioned her to me before, and I was glad to finally meet her.

"Just great!" He studied the bag she was carrying.

"These are for you because you've been looking so cold lately."

J.C. pulled out two beautiful striped wool sweaters that still had the store tags on them. He held them to his face like a newfound blanket. "This is amazing! Simply amazing, Nina! I can sure use these."

Nina's eyes lit up like tinsel. "My husband and I will be stopping by here next week some time before the holidays with the kids. They've been asking about you."

She waved, leaving a warm cloak of joy behind her.

"She seems really nice, J.C. You've known her a long time, haven't you?"

"Since the beginning, almost. She was pregnant with her triplets when she first started donating to me."

Holidays probably were hard for J.C., I thought, a time for reflection and also a time for regrets. He seemed to read my mind.

"I don't think I ever would have made it through the holidays if it hadn't been for the concern of my friends here," he said. "People

51

are so generous to me during the holiday season, both with donations and their time.

He was putting his new sweaters back in his bag when another cheerful hello emerged.

"Happy Holidays, J.C." A young man talked with him for a moment and handed him an envelope before he left.

"Look at this, Laurie." His face had a pensive yet content look. The card contained a gift of cash. He removed the cash and pointed to the writing. "No, this is what I want you to see. Read this." I read the card slowly, reflecting on the message of the holiday season. But the true gift was the simple note written on the bottom:

"Thank you so much for the joy you bring to me each day."

I could see why the holidays were a reaffirming time for him.

Peace is when time doesn't matter
as it passes by.
Maria Schell

8 Missing

The coldness of January was only going to worsen. I looked up
at the sky overflowing with clouds as gray as lead. The wind blew
through the buildings sending the frigid air through my layers of
clothing. J.C. hadn't been at his corner for almost a week. After
walking by his corner several days in a row, I was worried. I asked
the vendor on the street if he'd seen J.C. and he just shrugged his
shoulders. I kept walking by J.C.'s corner, visited the park, and
perused other blocks. No other street corners revealed any secrets to
me, although they were busy with others who walked like him. His
absence stood out like a tree that had lost its leaves. Even though the
wind whistled through the buildings and footsteps tapped along the
ice, I knew that it wasn't like J.C. to take so much time off.

"You said he was sick. Besides, homeless people move
around," my husband suggested.

"I'm worried, that's all." I brushed my hair out of my eyes and
looked at him intently. I began straightening up the magazines on the
coffee table and moved in front of the TV.

"If he's hurt or seriously ill, he might be at a hospital," T.J.
suggested. "You could start calling them."

I had thought about that but I didn't even know J.C.'s last name.
"I wonder if he's at a shelter?"

"I don't think you should go there alone, Laurie." T.J. met my
eyes, folding his hands on his lap in certainty. "It's not safe. If you
want, I'll go with you."

"No, I'll probably just call some of them." I made some phone
calls and I got in touch with a woman from Midnight Run, an

outreach group that comes into the city once a month and brings food to the homeless on the streets.[20] Sarah was her name, and she said she knew a J.C. Since I had a picture of him, I decided to go meet her and her van of volunteers.

It was a chilly winter night, and I hung around West 58th Street at 11:30 p.m. waiting for the van to get there. Men gathered at the block between Broadway and Eighth Avenue also waiting. My stomach twisted and churned with uncertainty until I saw a young couple standing off to the side and went over by them. They weren't homeless; they said they were just hungry.

As the van drove up, the men covered the curb like swarms of bees and a dark-haired woman jumped out of the van, bestowing hugs randomly.

"Sarah." My hopes lifted as I pushed ahead.

She studied the picture I gave her. "That's not my J.C. I'm sorry." She handed the picture back to me. "You'll find him, I'm sure. I'll ask everybody I know. Then I'll call you, okay?" She began to disperse food but left me with encouraging words.

But there was no news from Sarah.

I held my breath each morning as I turned the corner on Seventh Avenue. Ten days after he disappeared, relief fell through me like warm bath water when I finally saw his cups.

"Well, J.C., I'm glad to see you back!" My face was scrunched up and my breath was rushed. "I've been so worried about you, J.C.! "Where've you been?"

"Acapulco." He looked at me and laughed. "I'm just kidding. I wish I had been there."

I didn't say anything.

His face became serious when he realized my concern. "You know I've been sick. Remember, you told me I should take a few days off?"

I tightened my scarf around my neck and moved closer to the wall. "Yeah, but I didn't think you'd be gone this long! I walked by here every day looking for you, asked the vendors about you and even called several shelters looking for you." My words poured out

54

in concern. "But where did you go?" I wondered if he had been in the hospital.

"Just slept wherever it was warm. It wasn't so bad."

"Well, I'm glad you are okay." What does a homeless person do when they are sick? Staying in bed under warm covers and drinking hot tea wasn't an option. As I started to ask J.C., a slender, warm-eyed woman approached and stopped in front of us. "Welcome back, stranger. Are you all right? I haven't seen you here for awhile." That's how the morning continued. People who were worried about him stopped and donated even more generously than usual.

"You sure are loved by many people, J.C." I stood by him for quite awhile and was amazed at how many people stopped and talked.

He smiled bashfully. "It does feel kind of good, knowing so many people worried about me when I wasn't here. I have never missed this many days before."

"You know, J.C., I even contacted someone from the Midnight Run Outreach who thought she knew you. I went to meet her and some other volunteers late Saturday night to show her your picture."

"You what! It's not safe for you to be out alone at night."

"I know. I know. And it turned out she didn't know you. But she was very encouraging and helpful." I sighed heavily and met his eyes. "I just didn't know what to do." I added, "If you ever get in a situation where you need help, I want you to know you can always call me."

He nodded in appreciation. "Just be careful, Laurie. You know I worry about you all the time. You just don't know this place." He shook his head again. "Going out like that in the middle of the night. What were you thinking?"

He's probably right, I thought. "There were other volunteers there, J.C., and I felt safe enough."

He shook his head and touched my arm. "You never have to worry about me, Laurie."

I sighed deeply, thinking how a homeless person could just disappear and no one would ever miss him. "Well, promise me you'll call me if you ever get in a situation where you need help. Okay, J.C.?"

"Thanks, Laurie. I appreciate that more than you can imagine." He moved back and forth as if he were sitting on a rocking chair on a front porch of some old farmhouse. "But I'd never want to bother you."

Now that I knew he was okay, I was anxious to get back to interviewing. "So are you ready for our next interview, J.C.?"

"Any time you are. Just name the day."

We planned to meet again at the playground the next morning. I had some questions for him but really wanted him to just continue his story. I told him about paying him for his time and he was very pleased, I thought, not so much for the money, but for being treated like a business partner rather than a street person. I asked him once about how he dealt with people who ignored him day after day.

"I try not to take it personally," he told me. "My education helps me understand the psychology of why some people react like that. I don't hold anything against them. They have their reasons-- might be guilt, fear, or anger, who knows?"[21]

When I saw people begging on the street, I usually walked by quickly without looking at them. I read later, "Panhandlers elicit a range of emotions--from fear to anger, from resignation to pity--in the people they ask for help. *Donor anxiety*--what people experience when they pass by a homeless person. Each request requires a split-second moral judgment, an immediate answer to questions such as: should I give money to someone who might buy drugs or alcohol; is this person really homeless or simply begging; or why doesn't this person go to a shelter or soup kitchen?[22]

"But isn't it lonely, just sitting here for so many hours, J.C.?"

"You know, people can't believe I'm here every day. I bet I say 'Have a great one' at least a thousand times a day." He looked at the people passing by. "I have a lot of friends here now and talking to people is what I do best. Doesn't matter what color, age, sex, or class. I accept people for who they are. And there sure seems to be a demand for smiles, greetings, and well-wishes out here. So I give what I have to offer. It helps ease the loneliness." He sat quietly for a

56

few moments. "Away from this corner, though, I do get lonely. But here I can laugh, and I know the power of humor. I come here to get that."

One woman with soothing caramel eyes and cinnamon-colored skin polished like wood came up to him.

"Hi, J.C." Her smile spread across her face like butter, as she gently squeezed his arm.

"I'm sorry I haven't been giving money to you lately, but I've been having some bad times. I just wanted to let you know." The jagged sun between the buildings landed on her hair in shimmering lines.

"Don't you worry. You're paid in full." He laughed a quick smile and watched her face light up. "You have a lifetime membership with me! You take care of yourself first."

"Thanks, J.C. I will. Don't you worry about me." She lifted up her hand as she walked away. "Good luck to you."

J.C. glanced at me. "See what I mean. People are unbelievable!"

He's the one who was unbelievable, I thought with a smile.

The next morning I got to the playground before he did, which gave me some time to collect my thoughts. "J.C.," I began when he arrived, "will you tell me about shelters. I don't understand why you didn't go to one." I had been reading about shelters and had to admit that the newspaper articles were not very favorable.

J.C. sat back and held the microphone in his hand. He looked around for a few minutes, started to talk and then stopped when he saw someone close by walking his dog. I just waited, knowing he'd resume talking when he was ready. He started to talk and then stopped and turned off the tape recorder. "Before we begin. About this book. It's very important to me. I want to thank people, so many people that have given generously to me." A moment of silence passed. "If it weren't for them, I wouldn't be here today." His face seemed peaceful after saying that, and he turned the recorder back on. "Now, about shelters. . . .

Suffering breeds character, character breeds faith
and in the end, faith will not disappear.
Jesse Jackson

9 Go to a Shelter?

"Some shelters are good; some not so good." J.C. closed his eyes then sat up straight with wide eyes. "Let me first explain how it all works. You know, it's not so easy to get into a shelter. You've probably read stories about the intake centers where people wait for hours and hours only to find out they aren't eligible. You're not considered homeless if you're staying with relatives or friends.[23] Eventually, people learn how the system works. If a family can manage to survive on the streets for awhile, instead of staying with someone, it's to their advantage--they'll get into a shelter. Not that a shelter is what they want--it's assisted housing. But to get assisted housing, you have to be in a shelter first and get your name on a list. I don't know how long that list is but I heard it's a pretty long wait. Families get priority--which I think is fair--but the situation for homeless men is very dismal. After being determined eligible, a man who wants to move to assisted housing faces a longer wait.[24] But in the meantime, at least they don't have to sleep on the streets."

"So did you do this--go to a shelter so you could get on the list?"

"Well, Laurie, let me tell you. I was out of money. It was winter. My feet ached from blisters inside my stiffened socks. I knew I couldn't continue sleeping outside in this cold. So I visited some shelters. I could tell which shelters were the worst ones as soon as I turned down the street. I ended up first at the door of an old building covered with graffiti. People were sprawled out all over--some leaned stiffly against the building, some were sleeping or sitting on the sidewalk. One man's shoes had holes in them and I could see his socks, dried blood crusted on them from sores. Some men were twisted up and hunched over, wearing unwashed clothes, hands covered with dirt. The air reeked. A guard stood by the door and let me in when I told him what I wanted. I entered the darkened room, rows of benches like pews filling the front of the room, a small television up in the corner. Cots were lined up in rows in the back of the room. I breathed in a half-tobacco and half-mold stench."

I remembered when I had visited a shelter in Columbus. The room was dismal, and I remember the long tables and the sounds of men eating.

"A man wearing a wrinkled shirt sat by an old desk on the other side of a small window. He glanced at me quickly, looking me over in a quick assessment of sorts and asked if I had ever stayed in a shelter before."

"In that instant, my whole life seemed to pass in front of me as I realized how limited my choices were. I looked at the cots lined up on the floor, people alone and disoriented, resting with their bags under their heads, some covered with gray sheets and thin blankets."

"This guy pulled papers out of a folder and placed them in front of me and asked me for identification. When I set my backpack down to get my wallet out of my pocket, I sensed movement nearby. I turned to see a man running off with my backpack. I fled after him and pushed him roughly, grabbing my pack as he ran down the street."

"Someone just took your things while you were standing there?" I couldn't believe it.

"Yeah, you always have to be on the lookout, Laurie. That's why I'm always giving you advice about safety, you know. Well, I went back to the desk and then spoke loudly, 'I can't live like this.' I gestured to the dirty floor, the peeling paint on the walls, and the cobwebs above the door. The guy's mouth turned up slightly as if to say, 'Well, what can you do?' I was homeless, but I knew I didn't fit in here. I left with the smell of the shelter clinging to my clothes."

"I went to some other shelters after that, and didn't even like the ones that were cleaner and nicer. They'd hand me the list of rules and regulations, and I felt like I was back in school. A set meal time, assigned chores, and a curfew. Not for me. I couldn't live in a situation where my freedom was taken away. I was homeless, but I wasn't a criminal.[25] They had a policy of frisking everyone who came in for safety reasons, and I couldn't handle that. I went into one room filled with rows of tables. Cigarette smoke stung my eyes as I looked around. Men stood shoulder to shoulder getting their food, with little talking except for an occasional protest like, 'Hey, that's mine.' They shoved food inside their mouths, and food dropped on the floor. It stunk in there, and I left."

The more J.C. talked, the more I realized that he could never manage living in this kind of environment. "What about the private shelters?"

"Well, I went to a private shelter and women with kids filled the room. This particular shelter didn't allow men. The ones that did-- well, they had a long waiting list and requirements like attending church, Bible study, group counseling and so on."

"That doesn't sound so bad, J.C. Most homeless people need help or they wouldn't be homeless in the first place."

"Yeah, well I already had my Bible study with Reverend John-- I haven't told you about him yet. I just didn't like the idea of someone making choices for me. So I stayed on the street."

"What about work fare?"[26] I had heard about this relatively new program that was designed to help people get off welfare.

"It's enough money to keep you in the shelter but never enough to get you out." He paused for a second. "I could have done it, Laurie. I really thought seriously about it. But I would have eventually been thrown out. The crowded and unsanitary conditions were a breeding place for tuberculosis, lice, pneumonia, AIDS, and scabies. Who would want to be exposed to that?[27] I couldn't sleep next to drug addicts or criminals, and especially homosexuals."

He paused for a moment. "Not that I hold that against them or anything. I know it's a genetic thing. But the way I look at it, God put us here to multiply, and we both know homosexuality isn't about that! And I would have lost my temper the first time someone bothered me or my belongings. I'd probably end up in jail or a mental institution!"

I wondered how many others were like J.C.--living in an environment that only exacerbated their problems. J.C. knew himself better than anyone else. He knew his limits and that a shelter was not for him.

"At least on the street, I didn't have to talk to anyone if I didn't want to. I could avoid or walk away from bothersome people. But in a shelter, there's no place to go. You're stuck there!"

"So you just decided to stay on the street and sleep in the park?"

"Yeah, that's what I did. At least until it got too cold."

"You started sleeping on the subway then, right?" He nodded. "Tell me about the subway, J.C."

"It's awfully cold out here today, Miss Laurie." J.C. took off his gloves and rubbed his hands together.

"I know. We should finish up." I paused and collected my thoughts. "But I want to hear about the subways. How 'bout if we walk over to McDonald's and warm up with some coffee and talk there?"

I jotted down some notes while J.C. got us something to drink. I had already copied several articles about shelters, and now I was anxious to read them. I wondered if J.C.'s experience was typical or if he didn't really give it a chance. What else would someone do if they didn't have any place to stay and it was the middle of winter?

J.C. returned to the table with some coffee and continued talking.

> It is one of the most beautiful compensations of life,
> that no man can sincerely try to help another
> without helping himself.
> *Ralph Waldo Emerson*

10 A Routine to Follow

"Since I had noticed homeless people getting on the subway late at night, I got on and rode it from Battery Park to the Bronx. It was an hour's ride. Could close my eyes and nod off a little, catch some sleep. No one bothered me. The back cars were the best, less crowded, and no one rode in them late at night except other homeless people."

"So that's where you started sleeping?"

"Yep. I'd go to the subway, number 1, 9."

J.C.'s thoughts rolled into words as I listened to his story.

"I sat down on an empty bench and placed my bags on the floor. I learned by watching how others made the seat a bed, laying down pieces of cardboard and positioning their bags or packs under their heads. The men were all sitting up except for a longhaired man who lay sprawled on the bench across from me. One man, meeting my eyes, nodded, and I nodded back. The others appeared to be sleeping. I was the newcomer; the others had established this car as their turf, and I was intruding. Although I wanted to say something, a stillness hung in the air and I stayed silent. I needed sleep badly, but I couldn't relax, not knowing if I was really welcome in here or not. Occasionally my eyes closed, but for most of the night I just sat up and thought, watching the others carefully, checking them out, knowing that although their eyes appeared closed, they were doing the same. I went back there again the next night, and the same men were in the subway car."

"How late was it, J.C.?" My husband and I sometimes rode the subway late at night, but I didn't recall seeing any homeless people sleeping.

"Well, usually after midnight or so. But you see, the homeless only ride in the last car at night so they can sleep there without being bothered. Don't ever ride in the last car, Laurie. Not a good place for you, that's for sure."

"So did you just keep going there every night?"

"Well, I did but it took awhile before I felt comfortable. One guy seemed pretty friendly and motioned for me to sit on the bench across from him."

J.C. smiled for a moment. "He said to me, 'Welcome to the Holiday Inn.' This guy was more approachable than the others. It turned out we got off at the same stop in the morning and having that in common, started talking in a casual way. He told me the rules here-- stay away from the others, keep your belongings close to you and keep quiet. He told me I had to clean myself up and gave me an address of a place I could go. It turned out to be a crackhouse.[28] The room was cheap for the night, but I also had to pay for some crack and partake with the others to earn their trust. After a few nights of doing this, I was admitted through the door without any suspicious looks or questions. Even though I'd go back there every week or so to clean up, I tried not to get too involved in the drugs there."

"So I became a member of the subway car and those guys were friendlier to me. Got to know the guys and we shared stories, being careful to leave out the details. Can't be too careful, not knowing what someone might do with information you give out. The less known the better. We were all in the same boat; we needed sleep and we wanted to stay safe. We took turns staying awake without even discussing it. It was a silent contract we had and it enabled us to get some sound sleep every once in awhile."

"People rushed through the subway door in the morning and woke us up. Mornings were so hard; I didn't know how much sleep I actually got. My unconscious mind was always on guard and I never reached the place of deep sleep. I've never been much of a sleeper, remembering how the slightest noise, the crack of a twig, a rush of wind in the leaves brought me sitting upright in my bed. Vigilant, that's what the doctor said when mother took me in as a child, worried about me not getting enough sleep."

"My friend and I got off at 57th, and he stood by me while I got situated. When I first started panhandling, I'd stand for hours at a time but eventually found newspapers to sit on. I found a couple of plastic crates under the telephone booth and some sheets of cardboard from the nearby deli. I placed some behind my back to protect me from the cold brick building. I put my bags under the crate so my area looked organized. 'This is where I work,' I told him, 'and I don't want it to be dirty and messy."

"What was your friend's name?" This was the first time J.C. had ever mentioned a "homeless" friend.

"I just called him Joe, and that seemed okay with him. Anyway, I got my cups out of my bag and stacked them to a high. Joe chuckled as he watched people drop coins into the top cup and smile as they fell to the bottom. He stood over at the stoop next to me. I figured he probably wasn't ready to begin his day searching for cans. That's what he did, starting at the park, looking for cans and bottles in trash containers and under benches. Anyway, lots of people went by and gave me donations, and Joe just kind of stood there in awe. Reverend John, the one I'd been meeting several afternoons a week in the park for Bible study, talked to me for awhile."

"I remember when Joe said to me, 'How do you do it, Pops? Everyone loves you!' And he was right. 'Just being myself,' I said. And it was true. My parents taught me well, in an Emily Post kind-of-way. Good manners, always. Be respectful, appreciative, and make people smile. And always believe in yourself. No one could take that away from me. It went deep. Beneath my layers of clothing and the dirt of my skin, it was still there."

"You do have a certain charisma, J.C. Have you always been like that?"

"Oh, no! I remember my high school coach used to say to me. 'You got to start acting like a football star!' The truth was I avoided social situations as much as I could. People think that if you're in sports, you must have an outgoing personality. It took me quite awhile to come out from my shell, but I did. It was just a gradual thing. All those years of noticing and observing people, sitting back and taking it all in and finally I began to open up."

"So I depended on the only thing I had going for me--my personality. Couldn't make it happen. This was me when I had a job, made lots of money, owned a home and drove a nice car. Sometimes I'd wonder though, if I were such a great guy, how did I end up here?"

I was curious about Joe. "So what about Joe?"

"Joe hung around for awhile and then went to the park. You know, collecting cans can be lucrative for many homeless people. Joe was good at it. He was very thorough and patient and worked hard all day---got enough cans to bring him money for a meal. Stores paid five cents a can, a limit of 240 cans per person, but he said he never collected more than 60 or 70 cans a day.[29] He found a store that would take his cans as long as he came when the store wasn't busy. Sometimes Joe saved his money, and after a week or so, he had enough to rent a room for a night. Not for sleep so much, but for the shower. Joe told me his plan—had a bank account where he put his can-collecting money. Ate at soup kitchens to save money. Then once he got his social security check, he figured he'd have enough for a deposit on a studio apartment and then look for a job. He told me to check out my V.A. benefits but I already had. The paperwork, form after form, signature after signature. Wanted to know if I heard voices or if I was afraid of hurting anyone. They couldn't help me, said this was a treatment center and I seemed to be of sound mind. I had to say I was crazy and then they would help me. I wasn't crazy. I was homeless and maybe being homeless would cause me to become crazy. If so, then I'd go back. But not until then."

"What about you, J.C.? Do you have a plan?"

"Later. More about me later. Okay, Miss Laurie? Enough for today."

> Don't let what you cannot do interfere with what you can.
> *John Wooden*

11 Trying to Fit In

So J.C. had tried to get help, but his tolerance was very low. I wondered how many other homeless individuals weren't able to endure the stress of endless phone calls, long lines, and disrespectful treatment. It would be difficult to handle that stress since being without a home was enough of a challenge. Healthy individuals have difficulty coping with a crisis; how would someone with emotional problems manage to survive? Anger, depression, and anxiety would undermine their efforts to be resourceful.

J.C. was a very bright, articulate and personable man. Yet there were signs that he had some psychological issues that would hinder him from getting off the street. He was too proud to ask for help. He was very rigid in his thinking and needed to be in total control of his environment. He didn't have any network of support from family, friends, or the community. Perhaps the greatest deterrent to J.C.'s success was his distrust of others. Many of these characteristics were mild enough so that he could manage his homeless lifestyle but severe enough to keep him out of the mainstream of society. Yet, he had a gentleness about him, maybe an unrealistic view of the world, but his warm heart touched many people.

I spent the next few days gleaning through the news articles and books I had at home, as well as listening to J.C.'s tapes. I wrote up some of the key points about shelters and how it related to what I knew about J.C.

- Shelters deal with the symptoms, not the causes of homelessness. They isolate the homeless from the mainstream of society by taking them off the streets and out of sight. Shelters should be viewed as an emergency solution and not a permanent one.[30] *My question: Why wouldn't J.C. at least go there as a last resort--a place to stay until he could figure out what to do?*

- Shelters are so crowded that the nights are noisy with people talking, crying, coughing and so on. There's lots of nighttime activity, which may include drugs or alcohol.[31] *I couldn't picture J.C. in a shelter. He would not be able to deal with the noise and crazy behavior. He would stay up all night and watch others and protect his things. The lack of privacy would be devastating to him. He is a loner and would probably not socialize with anyone. He is so meticulous and orderly that the chaos and filth would totally unnerve him!*

- The Commission of Homelessness Report (1992) found that 65% of men in shelters tested positive for drugs. It was higher in city shelters--88%. However, many homeless turn to drugs after entering the shelter system as a way to numb themselves from reality.[32] Although shelters provide housing, homeless people depended on them for food and clothing, also, making it possible for them to spend what little money they had on drugs. *There wasn't any indication that J.C. was involved in drugs or alcohol at this time. I observed him to be alert, clear-eyed and coherent.*

- Shelters encourage dependency because independent decision-making is very limited. *J.C. liked to be in control and make his own decisions. He would have no patience with someone telling him what he could and could not do.*

- The lives of the homeless are devoid of everyday experiences such as planning meals, talking on the phone, watching television, and cleaning the house. Homeless people don't have this to fill their time so monotony and boredom result in listlessness or depression. The slow stretches of time that are uneventful and predictable lead to the rut of doing nothing. Shelters actually hide the homeless; the community doesn't have to deal with what they can't see.[33] *I never get the feeling that J.C. is bored or miserable, although when I ask him what he does with his time, he says he just comes to his corner or sleeps.*

- Lack of social interaction and isolation contribute to more boredom and loss of skills that are necessary to function in society. Living in a shelter is stressful, and because of deteriorating social skills and self-esteem, it is difficult for a homeless person to be successful on a job.[34] *J.C. would be annoyed and irritated with the behavior of others and keep to himself.*

- Research showed that assisted housing programs were successful. One current study suggested that the real problem was the city's scarcity of subsidized housing. This study challenged a widely held view that the most effective way to end homelessness among families is by first resolving such problems as mental illness and substance abuse. Yet over 80% of families, when provided with subsidized housing, remained stable despite their problems. Families, not wanting to return to shelters, are more motivated to get help for resolving their problems.[35] *Getting J.C. into some kind of assisted housing really seemed like a viable alternative because he already received Social Security. Yet, he insisted that the waiting period was so long, it wasn't worth pursuing.*

I thought this was also interesting. "Subsidized housing costs less than shelters. The Coalition for the Homeless put people into rent-subsidized apartments for only 1/3 of what it cost to run a shelter. A single bed in a shelter costs $23,000 a year; supportive housing costs $12,500 a year.[36] *J.C. had said the apartment he lived in before was affordable because it was city housing. Was this the same as subsidized housing?* Based on the literature I read, although shelters provided some short-term solutions, they just didn't seem to be the best alternative for all homeless individuals.

I had gotten so involved with my research that I hadn't seen J.C. for several days. He said he wanted to tell me about the time he was real sick and when he was robbed. "And then I have some surprises for you. Things that will blow you away."

"Like what, J.C.? Give me a hint."

"You'll see. Just be patient. I'll tell you when I'm ready."

I knew that even though he had told me a lot already, he probably was leaving information out. Maybe he was so evasive because he had to be to survive. All he had was his identity--where he went, where he slept, what he thought, and where he kept his things. For him to share that information with me was risky yet he maintained his trust in me. He probably told me more than he told most people.

> I love the man who can smile in trouble, that can gather strength
> from distress, and grow brave by reflection.
>
> *Thomas Paine*

12 Down Low, Moving Up

The frigid air claimed each day, the clouds slowly opening up like morning eyes, covering the ground with quilts of snow. The wind smacked my cheeks but I was content in my new coat. My coat was almost to my ankles and zipped up the front and tied tightly with the belt. It was like having a comforter wrapped around me. I pulled the fur-trimmed hood over my head and braved the cold.

"Well, hello Lady Laurie! You look as warm as can be today."

I smiled and shrugged my shoulders. "I love my new coat. But you know what Joey said? He told me I look like a grandma. He calls this my "grandma coat.""

"He said that! Well, I'll have to talk with Joey. You don't look like a grandma at all. You tell him that I said he has a very lovely mother!"

I laughed warmly. J.C. always knew the right thing to say. I settled back against the wall. "You look lonely sitting out here in this snowfall, J.C." I curled my fingers inside my mittens and noticed he was wearing several pairs of gloves.

"No, I think people worry about me in this weather. Donations have been good today." He gently shook his cup and the

70

coins clinked quietly.

"Well, you look pretty warm." I noticed the snow landing on his hat. "How's that hat working out for you?"

He laughed and told me how a woman had pointed to the earflaps of his hat and said he looked like the 'flying nun.'

"I told her that as I get older, being warm is a lot more important than how I look!"

I looked around and noticed that the streets seemed slow, the snow falling down at a faster pace now. "Let's go get some hot chocolate, J.C., and then you can continue your story."

We had developed a routine by now. At least a couple times a week we would get together and talk, beginning with my list of questions from previous interviews. J.C. seemed to handle my questions comfortably when I presented them in an organized way. He took a lot of time to answer each one the best he could. Then, if there was enough time, he just continued his story from where he had left off.

"Hey, before we begin, L.A., I got something for you." J.C. handed me a brown bag and added, "This is to show my appreciation for all the work you've been doing."

I had given J.C. a copy of the chapters I'd been working on. I assumed that's what he was referring to. But a gift of appreciation was a surprise! I pulled out a black leather organizer from the bag he gave me. "J.C. This is wonderful! I can really use this, you know!"

"I thought so. Hopefully, it'll help you keep your busy schedule organized."

I was touched by his thoughtfulness, and I told him so. I knew he didn't have the money to do this, yet he assured me he had made a good trade. "Things work a little different in the homeless world," he said with a chuckle.

"Well, thanks again." I gave him a long look and a warm smile. "Now, let's get started, okay?"

"Things had been going bad for me. The cold weather meant fewer hours panhandling, less money collected and less room on the subway. I kept to myself mostly for safety reasons, and the police didn't usually bother one homeless person. It got real lonely at times.

I met some people hanging outside the crackhouse, and every once in awhile, they'd slip me in and I'd get a chance to clean up. But I found myself spending more and more time there, no longer wanting to go back out on the streets. It wasn't too clean, but it was warm in there."

This was the second time J.C. had mentioned a crackhouse. I wondered if many homeless people ended up there. "What actually is a crackhouse, J.C.?"

"It's just a place to get drugs. It's that simple. And you can spend the night there--$50 a night. You'd be surprised how many homeless people use drugs, Laurie. Believe me, I was there. But it can ruin your life, that's for sure." J.C. sighed deeply and then looked at me, as if he was getting his thoughts together. "Anyway, they finally kicked me out. I wasn't even aware of how long I'd been there, or how long after that I slept on a park bench."

"I wandered the streets, feverish and coughing. I didn't have any money and when I tried to panhandle on my corner, even my regular customers backed away from me. I needed a shower, some food, and some clean clothes. I dug my nails into my skin, scratching and pinching the sores that were spreading. I changed into some clean clothes at a nearby church. My skin was a mess. My clothes touched my skin, and I cringed from the pain. I went back to the subway car to sleep and tossed and turned, waking myself with my own screams. I was miserable, and finally one of the guys said something to me so I went to the emergency room."

"J.C. Why did you wait so long to get help?"

"I wasn't of sound mind and body. Illness can do that to you, you know. I was still coming off the drugs, didn't eat properly, and was in constant pain. I was delusional a lot of the time."

"So as soon as I got in the hospital, the nurses rushed me into the shower, shocked by the bloody-pus sores all over me. They treated my hair and beard for lice, wrapped me in layers of towels, and applied cold compresses to my body. I was barely conscious as they started me on a schedule of shots and pills. I went in and out of consciousness for many days. After about ten long days, my sores started to scab over, and my fever subsided. I was sent back outdoors with some ointment, antibiotics and clean clothes."

"After that episode, I was meticulous about my hygiene. I started finding places where people were willing to let me stay until I had the money to pay them back. But it was hard to pay back that money. Even when my panhandling business got better, I couldn't get out of debt."

"My days at the crackhouse had set me back quite a bit. My body was weaker than before, and I needed the drugs for a lift. But when I tried to get back inside, they wanted money up front from me, said I owed them a lot already from my previous stays there."

"I had to get my strength back if I was ever to get back on my feet again. I decided to get some help. I called Susan and Charles. When I first started panhandling, they had given me their phone number and said I could call them if I ever needed help. So I called them. They walked with me to a hotel and paid for two nights. I had to stay clean; they understood that. It was a luxury to have a place where I could shower and wash out my clothes. It took me some time, but I picked myself back up again. I stayed away from the crackhouse and avoided the people that I knew went there. I isolated myself again, but I felt stronger, more focused, and hopeful."

J.C. sighed. "It was bad, real bad. Quite a scare to be that sick. And I had always been so health conscious before I became homeless. But I learned the hard way, and I've been healthy ever since."

I needed to review this new information so when I went home, I added it to J.C.'s timeline. The way I figured it, he was still in the first or second year of living on the streets. During this time, he used up the money he had, earned money by panhandling, went to V.A. services, found places in the park to sleep, found a subway car to sleep in the winter, got food and clothing from soup kitchens and churches, checked out several shelters, used crack, got seriously ill, and finally cleaned up his act. I just hoped he was being honest with me now and wasn't still involved in drugs.

He was a survivor, that was for sure. I wondered if living this way was a challenge to him--getting by with the minimal of help. He had always said he didn't like to impose on others, and he was definitely a loner. It was such a contrast from his life before--when he bought homes and cars and had a respectable profession. Yet, now he had none of the security that money and work could bring. Was he punishing himself for his irresponsibility of years ago? Was he trying to prove to himself that he could be homeless and survive? And since he had been homeless for so long, was he comfortable now just living this way?

There must be a homeless psychology, a unique way of looking at the world that is a resignation of some sort, where one gets accustomed to living in a simple way. The things that one might normally do throughout the day cease to be of any importance. Things fall away from one's consciousness in a gradual way--the only concerns are those that have to do with survival. Because of this, many homeless people lack the initiative to take care of themselves. The thought may be there for a moment or two, but it isn't acted upon, and there really isn't any stress because of it. J.C. seemed to need a push to get things done. After all, he had been living on the street for almost five years. The longer he was homeless, the easier it probably was to remove from consciousness those daily activities that needed to be attended to. Making a phone call, sending a letter, finding a bed, going to a soup kitchen, and picking up clothes at a church--all take a lot of effort. Many homeless people probably don't have the energy or motivation any more; and it becomes part of their lives to just sit and wait for things to happen.

I remembered what one of my contacts had said about the importance of understanding the homeless. So much depended upon the circumstances that led one to homelessness, whether help was available and if that person sought out help. Two profiles emerged among the homeless; those who sought help and who didn't. J.C. hadn't really pursued the avenues of resources available to him. Perhaps if he were more persistent, he would have gotten the support he needed to get off the street. Or maybe he would have kept getting frustrated and just given up, which was how he felt after he went to the shelters, the intake agency and the V.A. program.

Which leads to the next group of homeless--those who don't

really want any help. Either they want to solve their situation by their own efforts, or a drug/alcohol addiction or mental illness prevent them from seeking help, or they find homelessness a lifestyle they can live with. Certain personality types or those with emotional problems would fall into this category. J.C. had a distinct personality type. He had a charismatic personality, which served him well. He wanted to rely on himself, even if that meant panhandling as his means of support. Although he was relying on the donations of others, he was in control of his situation, making his positive panhandling image work for him. I was concerned about his emotional state, though. His independence, isolation, paranoia and need to be in control of his surroundings all supported his homeless lifestyle but were adversary to getting out of his situation. He said he didn't want to remain homeless, yet his own panhandling corner met his needs--financially, psychologically, and socially. I could see where it worked well for him this way.

I had originally identified him as someone I wanted to help, yet I wasn't so sure he really wanted the help. He said he did. Yet, it was as if he was just waiting for someone to come up and present him with a viable solution. The book idea was appealing to him for that reason--publish a book and then live off the proceeds. He could still be self-supporting and independent and be in control of his life. He wouldn't have to answer to anyone, wouldn't have the limitations of employment, and wouldn't have to interact with people he didn't want to. He could continue to make his own choices.

I was ready for him to tell me more. I wondered what else he had experienced--"Nightmare, Part II," as he called it. I was anxious to continue our interviews.

Things do not change, we do.
Henry David Thoreau

13 Nightmare, Part II

"So you were healthy again, no longer involved in drugs. Knew where to panhandle, eat and sleep. Things were looking up for you, weren't they, J.C.?"

"Yeah, I was ready to figure out what to do to get off the streets. I had had enough of being homeless. I needed to open a bank account and start depositing my Social Security check. I picked up my check each month at the Social Security office. As long as I had identification, I could get it cashed at a bank and use it to pay back my loans. But without proper identification, well, here's what happened." He stopped abruptly, and spoke in shortened words. "Nightmare. Part II."

"I'd been sleeping on the subway several months, feeling comfortable, too comfortable I guess. I must have been sleeping very soundly cause one morning I woke up and saw my backpack slit open and empty. I couldn't believe I had slept right through someone robbing me. The knife must have been only inches away from my neck cause I slept with my pack under my head. Not much remained but what upset me the most was that all my papers were gone. I had no identification. I looked around at the others, moving around, scratching their sides and shaking their heads, as if saying, 'Too bad,' and then busily checking their own belongings."

"I was at an all-time low after that. Not only was I homeless, but the last of my belongings were now stolen from me. I couldn't even prove who I was. I went on to my corner, and faces passed me in a blur. People seemed surprised that I didn't utter my usual greetings and some paused and looked at me intently before moving on. I felt like I was in a crowded room; the sounds of screeching brakes and blaring horns froze my thoughts. I wanted to plug my ears with my hands to make the noise stop. It was so deep inside me, and I couldn't silence it. I retreated into a crazy world where I couldn't even think."

"It hit me then. Really hit me. I'm homeless. Really homeless. My eyes teared up. My feelings were out of control. I wiped my cheeks while my other hand held the cups and people looked at me, not knowing what to say. That's when I saw Donald."

"Who's Donald?"

"Well, Donald started talking to me the first week I was out here. I appreciated his conversation more than anything else. He treated me like an equal, and we always laughed, sharing common stories. But I was shaking as I talked, finding it hard to tell him what had happened. He seemed to be at a loss for words, but he stood next to me for a long time and listened. 'You'll find a way, J.C.,' he said. 'I've known you a long time now and I know you'll work it out.' 'Not this time, Donald. I'm real down,' I told him. 'Hey, I bet you can't sit here for more than one minute without greeting someone walking by.' He laughed and elbowed me. 'Go on, try it."

"I realized I had still been nodding at people as they passed by, even as I sat here talking to Donald. He was right. I never stopped doing my job no matter what. I thanked him for his concern but Donald told me something I'll never forget."

"What's that, J.C.?"

"He said I reach out to people here when most people ignore what's going on around them. Told me that was my contribution, and I should never forget that."

"You really do, J.C. I'm glad Donald told you that. Did you feel better after that?"

"A little, the way you do when someone nods their head while you're talking and you know they're listening. He lifted me out of my craziness for a moment, but not for long. My eyes watered up, and my hands shook. Then Nina came by and saw me shaking. I repeated my story, explaining how all my things were stolen. Not just my identification but family photos, old newspaper clippings, addresses and phone numbers. Nina wanted to help somehow, but there really was nothing she could do. I did have a pretty good idea after talking to the others on the subway who had taken my things, but I knew I couldn't get to the two men who had my backpack. It wouldn't be safe for me--they stayed at one of the crackhouses, and I wouldn't be able to get through the door. Besides, they would have discarded most of my items by now, the things they didn't need. All they really wanted was my money, the little I had left."

"I felt better after Nina left, knowing I wasn't alone. But I was losing hope fast; I was running out of options. I thought saving money was unrealistic, but at least it was a plan. I was successful as a panhandler. This was my business, and I knew I'd find my answer here."

"So you decided to make panhandling your business, J.C.?

"Yes, indeed. You know, there are many homeless people who steal purses, sell drugs, or commit other crimes. You'd be surprised, Laurie. So I think my business is respectable, considering the circumstances. I call myself a 'Panhandologist'." He smiled. "And as soon as I made that decision, things got better for me. I took my work seriously, treating it as a job." J.C. spoke his words carefully, like a crisply starched shirt. "Think about it. I have excellent qualifications. I'm responsible, dependable, arriving every morning at 6:00 a.m. My absentee rate is low, and I am very respectful and personable. My business depends upon the impression I make on people so I don't push a shopping cart, hold up a sign, or do anything that could annoy others. I am very fastidious about my appearance, always conscious about wearing clean clothing and being well-groomed."

"Once I decided to panhandle on the corner of 57th and Seventh Avenue, my work habits fell into place. I had set hours and began to recognize the same people going by each day. I found I could count on my regulars to donate to me. I always treated them respectfully and appreciatively. They were, after all, my clientele."

"How long did you plan to continue panhandling? I mean, it can't be very lucrative."

"Well, I am one of most successful panhandlers in Manhattan. Next time we get together, I'll tell you about panhandling, Laurie."

Of course, I needed time to learn something about it on my own, I thought. So that's what I did.

Charm is the ability to make someone think you are both
good-looking and wonderful.

Unknown

14 Panhandling

Laws about panhandling changed in the 1990's in favor of the homeless. In 1993, a federal district court judge in the New York Circuit Court of Appeals ruled that panhandling was a form of free speech, protected by the first amendment which gave individuals the right to food, shelter, and clothing and the right to ask for help.[37]

When I asked J.C. about the laws, he said to ask the police, that they knew the laws better than anyone. He did say that panhandling wasn't allowed in the subway, in front of stores, ATM machines and busy public places.[38] Sidewalks remained open to panhandlers but not during lunch and dinner hours. And, of course, no harassment.

"What do you mean?"

"Like yelling at people, following them, cleaning their car windows. Stuff like that. As long as you don't create a nuisance, the police will usually leave you alone." Later, I found out that a ban against "aggressive" panhandling, as this was called by Mayor Guilliani, was signed into law in 1996. It was punishable by up to 16 days in jail and a $100 fine, and included blocking a pedestrian or car, using threatening gestures, touching or causing alarm or unreasonable inconvenience.[39]

"You definitely don't do that. I'm sure that's why people really treat you with respect," I observed.

"Yeah, but I've had my share of people who don't like having me here."

"Why? What happened?"

"It was getting harder and harder to sit out there each day in the cold weather. I felt embarrassed wearing so many layers of clothing, but I needed to keep warm. I noticed other homeless people panhandling inside the subway station, some singing, playing instruments, or just holding out a cup. There weren't any panhandlers down in the subway at my corner so I decided to move downstairs where it was warmer. I stood at the bottom of the stairs, holding my cups, smiling and delivering greetings."

"My regular customers were fine with me being down there. Like Janzeen. She had been talking to me a few months and took me to breakfast at least once a week, encouraging me to be positive and not give up. Being homeless, I felt isolated a lot, and I missed not being able to talk to people on the same level as myself. I always looked forward to seeing her. But not everyone liked having me there."

"Why, J.C.? What happened?"

"This one nasty guy said, 'I have to go out in the cold every day. So should you!' A policeman said to me later that this guy was complaining about me asking for money. I got very irritated. This policeman knew me and kind of looked out for me. He knew I didn't bother people. But he said it would be a good idea for me to move back outside. About this time, there had been some new rulings about panhandling, and police had begun to clear panhandlers out of the subway. I realized he was just doing his job, and I didn't want to cause any trouble. I moved back outside, adding more layers of clothing to keep warm."

"I'll never forget what that guy said to me when he saw me the next time. He said, 'I see you finally got your black ass out of there!' I met this man's eyes. He walked away with a smirk on his face and I stared at him in disbelief. I couldn't understand his animosity toward me."

"Did he stop bothering you after that?"

"Yeah, but I still see him walking by. He just ignores me now." J.C. paused for a moment. "I just swallow my pride a lot. It's easier that way. Some people aren't tolerant of panhandlers, and although they may donate to me one day, the next day they may yell at me. I've gotten some nasty comments, like 'Get a real job!' or 'Do something meaningful.' One guy said to me, 'You look like an idiot! Get rid of those cups!' and he knocked them over. It's hard to ignore this stuff, and it makes my job difficult at times."

"Do you ever just yell back at people who treat you like that?" J.C. didn't seem to me to be the kind of person that would just sit there and take it.

"Sometimes. Yeah, sometimes. But I have a hard time with my temper, and it's better for me just to ignore it and walk away. I just have to do that sometimes, you know." He looked pensive as he said that, and I thought that maybe his temper had gotten him into trouble before.

"When I first started panhandling, it took awhile for me to earn the confidence of the police in the area. Once they realized that I was respectful and polite, they began looking out for me. The police have become my strongest allies. They noticed immediately what kind of effect I had on this block, watching me as they walked and drove by, and I came to know them by name. Policemen in uniform, plainclothes policemen, and detectives all greet me warmly. They look out for me, I know. Once I was sitting here, and a drunk man was bothering me, angry about being robbed, and started questioning me about my belongings. It wasn't long before a plainclothes policeman noticed the man and asked him to move along, 'Don't bother J.C.,' he said. Another time I was sleeping on the subway and woke up suddenly to see five or six transit policemen standing over me. They said I was screaming in my sleep and were checking to see if I was okay. The police here in Midtown and Central Park are the best in the city!"

"I always worry about safety. I don't have much, but I'm very cautious about rummaging through my bags while I am sitting here. Someone might see my things and try to rob me later. Nowhere is really safe for a homeless person. It's all about becoming "street smart," and I have to look out for myself. I'm constantly aware of what's going on around me. I've become somewhat paranoid-- always ready for the unforeseen, ready to move or act. I can tell by the way someone walks or the look in their eyes if I can trust them or not. Although the police patrol the streets and parks, things can happen so fast. After living on the streets for so long, I never let my guard down. It's so ingrained in my personality, that I don't know if

82

I will ever be able to live in a relaxed way again. I naturally isolate myself because I like my privacy, but mostly for safety. I don't know who I can trust out there. So I've become suspicious of everyone. I don't want to get burned again."

I had been curious all along as to how much money he actually made. I saw him get dollar bills more often than he got change. "Is your panhandling business good, J.C.?"

"It's taken me lots of time to build a clientele. The first few months I'd sit out all day and end up with only $3.00. As people got to know me, my earnings increased. On bad days, I may only collect $5.00 or so. Twenty dollars is a good day. I also receive very generous donations on holidays. I keep the bills in my pocket and let the coins fill the plastic bottle at the bottom of the cups. I empty the bottom cup once in awhile or people will see it full and might think I don't need anymore money! When I first became homeless, I would go to soup kitchens and churches to get food and clothing. But now I enjoy choosing my own food, and I'm more able to afford it. Although I receive clothing from my regular clientele, I still need to purchase many items myself." He grinned widely. "I'm a real entrepreneur! I use marketing strategies--I've chosen the best location, and I use my people skills.[40] But although my business does well, panhandling just isn't a good way to plan for the future. The most I'm able to plan for might be that day only, especially since money can get lost or be easily stolen."

"So what is your secret of success?"

"Well, first my cups. Then people see beard and my smile and then they hear my words. From there it's up to me. It's in my hands." He thought hard for a moment, then said, "Creativity. But without bringing too much attention to myself. I don't want to cause any kind of commotion at my corner or the police won't let me stay. I thought about playing the saxophone, juggling, putting lights on my cups, or wearing a suit or a costume. I try new things ever so often. Once I found a desk chair by a dumpster and brought it over to my corner and sat in it. People laughed. Then I got another one and put it in front of mine, as if I was interviewing someone. One man offered me twenty dollars for the chair so I sold it to him! This year for the first time I had a plastic pumpkin full of Halloween candy on the sidewalk in front of me. On Valentine's Day, I had a large red balloon tied to one of my mail bins. For Easter, I had a basket full of candy kisses. I do these things mostly because of the response I get. I try to make people laugh."

"Common pitches of panhandlers like 'Do you have any change?' or 'Help me get something to eat' don't always work. People respond better if I don't pressure them. They know what I want. I won't insult their intelligence or put them on the spot. They might walk by me the first couple times, but they remember I didn't bother them. I've had people walk by me, turn around and look at me several times, only to come back and give me a donation." He met my eyes with a mischievous grin. "Like you did, Lady Laurie!"

He was really on a roll talking about this. He knew panhandling well. I was so intrigued at how proud he was of himself as he talked. I would think that panhandling would be embarrassing for him, and yet he treated it as a viable occupation.

"I watch out for others too. I notice when someone needs help. I might catch someone's arm if they trip coming up these stairs. Actually, one morning a well-dressed elderly man did just that. 'He slipped and fell,' I said to a nearby vendor, motioning to this man leaning against the building. I got some ice and held it on his forehead until he calmed down." He thought for a moment. "I also help mothers carry their strollers up and down the steps. And sometimes I'm just a New York tour guide, giving directions to stopping tourists. I'm even a messenger--asked to relay messages to other people."

He lowered his voice. "I remember once a friend gave me some change and as I watched him walk away, I saw someone was following him. I noticed his wallet in his back pocket and knew what was happening. I left my things and ran hurriedly until I caught up with him. I told him to put his wallet in his shirt pocket. He looked at me funny and then the next time he passed by my corner, I explained what happened. 'I just couldn't sit here and do nothing,' I said. 'I knew you were going to be robbed."

84

"Many other homeless people know of me and are curious about my panhandling success. If they are sincere, I give them advice about panhandling. But when they stand by me, it detracts from my business. I'll give them some of my change or food so they'll move on. One time a homeless man was sitting here on my corner when I arrived one morning. He knew this was my station--he left right away, without me having to say anything! I try to be pleasant, but protecting my turf always takes precedence. I take great pride in this corner and don't want other homeless people to detract from it."

J.C. stopped talking. "Could you do me a favor? Stay here and watch my things while I go to the restroom?"

"Yeah, go ahead, J.C. I'll keep an eye on your things."

He went down the subway stairs, his shortcut over to the park. I held his cups for him and felt a little self-conscious as people looked at me. J.C. should really write a guide for homeless people who want to panhandle, I thought. I smiled as I thought of his resourcefulness. He seemed to enjoy himself so much here. He was in his element-- conversing with people, using his charm and his outgoing personality. And people treated him so kindly and so respectfully for the most part, I wondered if he would really ever want to leave this corner. He said he did, and I believed him, but I knew that he would miss this, this notoriety of being the best panhandler around!

When J.C. came back, he continued talking where he left off. "I didn't tell you about Rob, did I?" I shook my head.

"Rob would come by every day or so. He worked here, cleaning the streets. He always talked to me, even though he was kind of shy. One day I was feeling kind of down in the dumps, and was going to finish up panhandling early. The street was busy as usual, people tumbling out of the subway like clothes in a dryer. Rob was sweeping the sidewalk near me, but today he was sniffling and wiping his eyes. I asked him what was wrong and asked if he wanted to talk about it. I motioned over to the step nearby and we sat down. I gave him a napkin from my pocket for his runny nose. He told me he had just gotten called at work; his father had just passed away. 'I wish it wasn't true,' I told him, 'but we all die some time.' I told him that he's still with him inside--not to forget that ever. He told me stories with words that spoke of his closeness to his father. When he got up to leave, his eyes looked clearer. He thanked me for talking with him. I was just glad I could help."

I didn't say anything; I just watched J.C.'s face, still and smooth.

"I still see Rob almost every day now. We kind of have a special bond." J.C. sat quietly for a moment. "You know, those sad feelings never really leave. I can still almost see my mother's face when I close my eyes."

It was true; some people are always with us, reminding us of our blessings. I thought about my Aunt Mary, and Grandpa--two vibrant, life-loving spirits. Their energy would always be with me.

J.C. changed the energy on this corner--a kind of magic that wrapped around you like a fur coat. I couldn't understand how he could do this every day, but he was so proud of how he handled his "work"--his panhandling business. He saw himself providing a service.

"But I want this to be my last year on the street," he said. "I can't keep it up. It's too hard on my back and my overall health sitting outside in this kind of weather."

"What are you going to do, J.C?"

"I'm waiting for someone to recognize my potential, see that I'm worth their investment. I just want to get my life back."

It seemed like a simple enough idea. But did he really believe that this would happen—that someone would just come along and give him a lot of money? Maybe a job, but money?

A few days later J.C. said to me, "I figured out what kind of job I want to get."

"Oh yeah? What's that?"

"I'll be your chauffeur!" His grin covered his face.

I had to laugh. "You mean, like 'Driving Miss Daisy?'"

"Yeah, like that. You know, drive you and your family around."

I could picture J.C. sitting in front of a steering wheel, dressed in a black suit and fine hat, smiling and making a commentary as he drove around. "Well, J.C., that would be great, but you know what?

You're going to have to find someone that can afford a chauffeur, and I'm afraid that's not me!"

I spent the rest of the day at the library; I wanted to read some more about panhandling and find more information about the homeless in NewYork City. I copied some interesting articles and I was getting more familiar with the jargon. My notes:

- *Compassion Fatigue*--the buzz word coined in the 1980's in San Francisco, described as "the cumulative effect of no longer wanting to deal with the misery on city streets. Many Americans now see the homeless as responsible for their own fate."[41]

- *Quality of Life*--Mayor Guilliani promoted his "quality of life" policy in New York to keep the homeless out of sight, through city sweeps.[42] In 1989, former Mayor Koch made a serious plea urging people not to give on the street anymore, portraying them in a despicable way.[43]

- News media--A drop-off of local and national coverage of homelessness has contributed to the public's change in attitudes. In ten years' time, the *New York Times'* articles about the homeless went from 50 to 10. In *Newsday,* the number of stories decreased from 88 to 27.[44]

- *Deserving and undeserving poor*--The distinction is made between the "deserving poor" and the "undeserving poor," the former those who can't work and deserve charity, and the latter those who can work but don't, and therefore, are punished.[45]

I questioned my own reactions to homeless people--did I look away and move aside or avoid a certain corner or give looks of disgust, annoyance, or anger? Did I ever say something insulting? Did I feel guilt, fear, or compassion? How often did I give change, say hello, or make eye contact, or smile? Could I feel their pain when I looked into their eyes?

Although a large number of homeless people still are on the streets, a feeling of invisibility pervades as they are ignored. A disturbing quote I read depicts this attitude--

"Why not create a beggar-free zone somewhere in the city.... then hardworking, taxpaying citizens can come to this zone to shop, eat out, or go to a movie without the fear or dread of being harassed by this human waste."[46]

Yet, how is panhandling any different from the charitable solicitations on the street corners by agencies like the Salvation Army? How can we be sure that that money is going for the causes we want to support? Some people would rather have more control in determining where their money goes. Why not give money directly to the homeless person instead of the agency? But then one has to wonder how this money will be used.

It is aesthetically unappealing to see people living on the streets, but more than that, it is unbelievable that in the abundance of our society, many people just barely survive. J.C. told me about a man from Australia who stopped and talked with him, and as he left he gave him a one hundred dollar bill, remarking to him with deep conviction in his eyes, "It's a disgrace that a city this size does not take care of their own."

I had learned that there are many resources available to help those who want help. Are those self-directed individuals getting the help they need? If so, then the focus needs to be on helping those who, for whatever reason, do not help themselves. Are we responsible for those people, or should we just let them learn the hard way? But then one has to ask, "What if they don't ever learn?"

Always do right. This will gratify some people
and astonish the rest.
Mark Twain

15 On the Street Where You Live

The subway stopped, and the doors opened. People rushed out and pushed in with the hurriedness of cattle. I hadn't ridden the subway with the work crowd before and moved quickly to get inside. The person in front of me wouldn't budge, although I could see there was room next to her. I squeezed in before the doors closed and held my bag over my head to keep from losing it in the door.

I was really getting fed up with the rudeness in the city--people not moving out of the way, completely oblivious to anyone else. Later that morning, a man walked by me holding a large box and accidentally ran into my shoulder. I yelled, but he kept walking without an apology, only a backwards glance. I wasn't in a good mood anyway after what J.C. did.

Yesterday he said, "You know I'm smart, don't you?"

"Of course, J.C. No doubt about it."

"3905."

"What?" I didn't understand what he was saying. A number?

"3905. That's your apartment number."

I was shocked. "How do you know that?"

"I told you I was smart. I can find out almost anything I want."

I was outraged. "What business is it of yours? Why would you want to find out where I live? It's a matter of privacy." I went on and on. "If I wanted you to know where I lived, I would tell you. Now I have to worry about safety."

"That's the last thing you have to worry about. I'm more concerned about your safety than anyone, Laurie."

"I am so upset about this, J.C. I can't even talk about it." I felt violated. How could he have ever found out? Did he have someone follow me into my apartment building? Or worse yet, was there someone waiting in the hallway? My thoughts moved in circles, making my head spin. "I have to leave, J.C. I can't even talk about this now." I walked away without looking back.

I felt like he had overstepped his boundaries. He could have easily followed me to see what building I lived in. But the doorman didn't let anyone in unless they lived there. How did J.C. get my apartment number? I couldn't figure it out. I was always careful to lock my apartment door now and walked around observing the people around me. I stopped visiting J.C.

I spent the next few days questioning if I still wanted to help him. If actions are motivated by a payoff, or a desired consequence, what was the payoff in this situation for me?

My friendship with J.C. was becoming a journey through my own feelings about helping the homeless but also was giving me a chance to look at my own issues. I was sensitive to J.C.'s needs. But where was I to set the boundaries on the amount of help I could give him that would be beneficial to him and at the same time not hurt me? I wanted to believe he was a helpless victim, and I was going to rescue him. Why was this agenda so important to me? Why was I so attracted to helplessness? Was it because I always had to work so hard for what I got, and I didn't want others to have to do the same? Yet I did, really. I'd get so upset when people didn't help themselves.

I'd always been vulnerable to people who were nice. And J.C was just that. I liked the attention I was getting from him. But sometimes my vulnerability got me into difficult situations, and I'd ignore the doubts inside me. I wanted to protect my belief that he was sincere and that he could be trusted. Why did I want to protect his image? Did my belief in him reflect on me--if I was wrong about him, would that mean there was something wrong with me?

What was J.C.'s motivation for finding out my address? Was he simply curious or just genuinely concerned about me? Maybe it was about the issue of control--the more information he had at his disposal, the more confident he'd feel about his environment. My husband thought that J.C. probably just wanted to show me that he was clever. I didn't have the answers to these questions, and I went around and around in circles trying to decide what to do.

"I just wanted to know in case you ever needed help and I'd know where to go," he said apologetically the next time I saw him. "I'm sorry to have upset you so much." J.C. was only doing what he thought was best. The challenge for me was to decide what I thought was best--not just for him, but also for me.

I have striven not to laugh at human actions, not to weep at them, nor to hate them, but to understand them.

Benedict Spines

16 Taking Care of Business

"Boy, my funds are low this week. I need some cash." J.C. started fiddling around with his things, pulling papers out of his pocket.

"But it's the first week of the month." I knew that he must have just gotten his Social Security check.

"My check's almost gone." He sighed and saw my eyes harden. "Since I don't have I.D., the place I cash it at takes a nice profit."

I didn't understand. "I thought you were going to open a bank account." We had talked about this before when he told me his I.D. had been stolen for the second time, and he needed an address to open a bank account. I gave him the name of a church that arranges for homeless people to use their address for mail delivery. "Did you check out that church?"

"Yeah, but I'm not crazy about having my mail go somewhere like that. Anybody has access to it; my mail wouldn't be safe. Besides, I can't open an account without identification anyway."

I had an uneasy feeling about this. "J.C., I feel like you are asking me for some money and I can't give you any." I paused and added, "You know it is up to you to decide if it's important enough to have a place to cash your check and if the risks outweigh the benefits." He looked at me with complete attention. I continued to make my point. "Your Social Security check is your main source of income. How much do you lose each month?"

"About $80.00. That's what they take."

"That's money that could have been in your hands instead of someone else's." I paused for a second and waited for him to respond.

"Well, I guess I need to get my I.D. replaced. I've been putting

92

that off."

"Well, I can help you write a letter requesting a new birth certificate, okay?"

He nodded his head.

"We'll get going on that right away."

It was becoming clearer to me that J.C. had difficulty dealing with things I viewed as simple matters. Getting stolen I.D. replaced was seen as a long, grueling process and that was stressful for him. All I could do was break it down into manageable steps for him and hope he'd follow through.

I sent away for J.C.'s birth certificate, which arrived in a few weeks. "Now, you're all set. What's the next step?"

J.C explained what he had to do--go to Motor Vehicles and get a picture I.D. "I need one--for check cashing, for a bank account. You name it." After waiting in the long line at Motor Vehicles, he found out that he did not have the necessary documents to get a photo I.D. card. Each piece of documentation was awarded points and even though he had his social security card, birth certificate, Medicare card and Veteran's card, he still didn't have enough points. He told me he was very frustrated and discouraged.

After studying the document list, he decided that a passport would afford him the most points. But the passport office required picture identification. A signed affidavit from someone who had known J.C. for at least two years was acceptable. I couldn't help him there.

"This is the only way I can get a passport. I hate to ask people to do this; people are funny about stuff like that. I already mentioned it to two people who have known me for at least two years, and they said they'd think about it. They never got back to me with an answer."

"Gosh, J.C. Is there anyone else you can ask?"

"Hmmm." He scratched his head for a moment. "Did I ever tell you about my lawyer?"

"Lawyer?" He has a lawyer, I thought. How could that be? But J.C. never failed to surprise me.

"You know, since I've been homeless, some extraordinary

things have happened to me. Being sent to this corner and not a different one. Meeting Nina, Donald, and you. And James Greer, my lawyer. Somebody's doing something. It's miraculous, really. God has to have something to do with it."

J.C. had referred to his faith in God numerous times, and I sensed that he had deep religious beliefs. I kept quiet, waiting for him to continue.

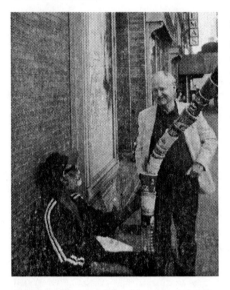

"Yeah, my lawyer. My pro bono lawyer. Greatest guy around. He's retired now; wasn't when I first met him. He knows me better than anyone else, except for you now." He looked at me with a slight smile. "He's helped me out a lot." J.C. moved his eyes back and forth.

He was thinking. Should I wait for him to continue or ask? I decided to ask. "How has he helped you?"

"He's always been very generous to me, never forgets me. Especially on holidays. But it's his concern, his genuine concern for me that I appreciate. He said to me once, 'No matter what your story, J.C., no one should have to live like this.'"

J.C. looked up quickly. I started to ask him a question, but he gently touched me on the arm. "Shhh. See how the fruit man just moved over here. He's listening to us." J.C.'s voice quieted down. "Yes indeed, the weather's been fine lately." He continued to make small talk until the fruit man left. "Always look around and see what's happening. Never forget that, Laurie. I'm telling you. I know about these people."

I wanted to tell him that I didn't think the fruit man was much interested in our conversation, but in order to get back to discussing

94

his lawyer, I continued quietly, "Now, you were saying about your lawyer . . .?"

J.C. nodded.

"He came by one day and grasped my hand tightly. This is a good man, a holy man, I thought. I wasn't surprised when he said he wanted to help me out, but first I had to prove that I was who I said I was. He was a lawyer, after all. I told him that might be a problem, since all my identification had been stolen, but he said to write the necessary letters and replace what I could. 'Let me know when you have your I.D.,' he said. I don't know why he trusted me. Here again, I thought, this is miraculous."

"A friend of mine, Bridgett, wrote the letters for me and I got my birth certificate, Social Security card, and Veteran's card. Took some time but after I finally received these documents, James was convinced. It was all here in print. He told me to look for an apartment and he'd help me out with the deposit and first month's rent."

"I found an apartment reasonably cheap, but my Social Security check still wasn't enough to cover it. James paid the deposit and the first month's rent and helped me find some used furniture. The plan was that I would use my panhandling money to make up the difference. It seemed doable."

"Four years, four long years of living on the streets and now I had a roof over my head, a door to close, a bed to sleep in. Each small convenience in my apartment, all the things I used to take for granted--hot water, plates, a toilet, doors, windows to open, a place for my belongings, a place to lay my clothes to dry, a pillow, a refrigerator, a stove--each day I thanked God for giving me my life back."

"When was this, J.C.?" I needed to put this all in perspective-- his life was so confusing sometimes.

"Oh, late 1997 I guess," he hurriedly spoke.

"The first few nights I tossed and turned, feeling like something was wrong. It was too quiet, too comfortable, and too clean. I had gotten used to a different way of life, nights filled with noises, bodies, and odors. But when I was finally able to relax, how I slept!

It was hard to get myself moving in the morning. Walking away from a hard bench was a whole lot easier!"

"I kept panhandling each morning, feeling somewhat guilty to be getting money this way since I wasn't homeless anymore. But I wasn't ready to start looking for a job yet. I needed time to adjust to my new life. I needed to think about the kind of work I wanted and was qualified to do. I didn't have work clothes, and my self-confidence was pretty shaky. But I was happier now than I had been in a long time. James stopped by to check on me and even paid my electric bill. He was the only one who knew about my apartment. I appreciated his help so much, but more importantly, I knew that he had enough faith in me to extend his generosity in this way."

I waited to see if J.C. was going to continue. An apartment--he had an apartment! Did he still have it, I wondered? He seemed to read my mind.

"And as we speak right now, that's where I am."

I was speechless, my heart surging like an elevator to the bottom floor. All these months I had worried about him living on the streets, and he had been living in an apartment! I remembered once talking to T.J. about giving J.C. enough money to stay at a hotel for a week during those below zero temperatures in January. Everything I did was in good faith, believing that he really had no choice about his situation.

I found my voice somehow. "You mean all this time, you've been sitting at the corner and you're not really homeless?" My face tightened up and my lips pursed together. He'd been living in this apartment for over a year, yet still considered panhandling his job.

"I had to keep panhandling. I didn't have enough to live on," he continued.

"Well, did you try to get a job?"

He just kept saying he needed more time, he wasn't prepared. Maybe he didn't have that drive or resourcefulness to move ahead. Or had the panhandling gotten so comfortable that he wasn't willing to give it up? Maybe it was that difficult to find a job at his age. But there had to be another reason why he was reluctant to work. Did he have a bad record or a blemished work history? Was he sick, mentally unstable, drug or alcohol dependent?

"So a couple months went by and the people that I owed money to started tracking me down. I owed a lot of money. Over the course of four years, fifty dollars a night several times a month, really adds up. When I started paying back the money, I got behind in my rent. I didn't want to bother James again. He had helped me enough already. Most of my Social Security check went toward the loans. People kept saying that if I could afford an apartment, I could afford to pay them money. They wouldn't take no for an answer. I knew I'd probably be back on the street again soon." He paused for a long moment. "There's more, Laurie. Now that you know about the apartment, I want to show you this." He handed me a piece of paper. The word that jumped off the page was "eviction."

I looked at him with questioning eyes.

"I wasn't able to pay the rent. The landlord caught up with me. And this is where it stands now. Actually, I've been lucky to have had the apartment for this long."

Now I understood why the idea of a book appealed to him. Here was a chance for him to get the money he was looking for. But was an easy way--he didn't have to work, he could sit back and let the money come in. Did he feel that he had dug a hole so deep that this was the only way out?

But he didn't think like me. I had to accept this and realize the decisions he made were guided by different life experiences than mine. All this time, I had been trying to help him by imposing my own values on him. But the thought processes of a homeless person couldn't be equated to those of the rest of society. J.C. had a way of looking at things totally unlike most people I knew.

I needed to talk to someone who could give me some insight. I called Sarah from Midnight Run and told her everything I had learned about J.C. and how I felt betrayed by him.

"The apartment gives J.C. a place to get out of the cold, a bed to sleep in. No more than a temporary place to stay. That's why he didn't look for a job. He knew he'd be evicted eventually and when that happened, he'd deal with it. He's a survivor." Sarah had worked with the homeless for so many years; she was a high school teacher, but her dedication to the homeless was like a second job to her.

"But J.C. wants to get off the street for good. Why can't he see the hole he's digging for himself?"

"A homeless individual has difficulty forming long-term goals. Each situation is dealt with as it arises--kind of like crisis intervention. Someone becomes homeless and remains homeless because they need to shut themselves down to the intricacies of their lives. They find solace in the streets where they don't have to deal with a job, family, or community obligations. The longer one remains homeless, the harder it is to re-enter society. J.C. has made this lifestyle work for him; each decision he makes is carefully calculated to solve an immediate problem. A homeless person has to be very shrewd."

"I just don't know what to do, Sarah. I feel like he's manipulating me."

"He is, but he doesn't see it that way. You are another solution to the crisis he faces. That doesn't mean he doesn't care about you. It's just that survival is the most important thing to him."

I remembered that J.C. had once said that everything went back to that instinct of survival. And he had found the means to survive all these years.

"He sees the book as a panacea for his ills. In his eyes, this will solve all his problems. But he will eventually end up on the streets again if he doesn't get help with his emotional problems. A friend of mine who used to be homeless says it's a constant battle keeping his wits about him, in spite of all the therapy he has undergone." Sarah paused and sighed briefly. "You may not be able to help J.C., not if he doesn't want to help himself. All you can do, Laurie, is be there in the best way you know how. Just knowing you care means a lot to J.C. It's probably a rare experience for him to trust anyone. Just don't let him manipulate you into doing something that won't be good for him in the long run. And that's easier said than done."

Talking to Sarah helped me feel like I wasn't losing my mind. Her experience gave her a realistic view of the problems of homeless individuals, and as we continued to talk, she shared some of her success stories, but also talked about some of the people she couldn't help.

I felt like a weight had been lifted off my shoulders, as if I had finally solved an algebra problem after hours and hours of hard work. I had a clearer perception of J.C.'s problems, and the anger and frustration that I felt for so long began to dissipate. I accepted J.C. at the place he was at. Each step I took with J.C. challenged my thinking and forced me to deal with my emotions. I was frustrated but not ready to give up yet.

The true test of character is not how much we know how to do,
but how we behave when we don't know what to do.
John Holt

17 Housekeeping

J.C. and I spent a lot of time trying to figure out what he could do after the eviction. He told me about how he got an extension through the courts, and would try to hold off the eviction until he had another apartment. I couldn't understand how he was able to do this, but it was something I let him take care of.

I met with Mr. Greer, his lawyer, and we discussed his situation. "Your lawyer doesn't understand about the "loans.""

"What's not to understand," J.C. said, giving me a perplexed look.

I didn't answer but continued, "He did say he would help you get a passport since he has known you longer than two years. And he offered to pay for it, but first he wants you to get your passport picture taken."

"Good, very good. I knew I could count on him." J.C. smiled and clasped his hands together.

"You know, J.C., I'm willing to help you out but I want to be sure you don't default on your rent again." I paused and looked at him straight in the eye. "You have to do your part. There's a limit to what I will do." I let my words sink in for a moment. "It is important that we have trust in each other, in order for our friendship to be sincere. I am genuinely concerned about you, but this is a two-way street. You may never have someone who is so willing to help you get on your feet to this extent again. And I have to tell you, sometimes I feel like I am being used."

He looked at me very intently as if surprised that I felt that way. "I would never use you, Laurie. You gotta believe that. I respect you too much." He continued in earnest. "I know that I have to do my

100

part. I can't believe sometimes that God is giving me another chance." I could see his eyes through his dark glasses, and I saw that he heard me loud and clear.

In light of my discussion with Sarah, I kept in mind that his definition and my definition of "being used" were probably very different.

I asked him the next few days if he had gotten his passport picture taken. He always had an excuse, and I confronted him on it.

"J.C. You are not doing your part. Your lawyer is waiting for me to call him, but I have to see the picture first. What's the problem?"

J.C. looked at me for a moment. "It's just not that simple, Laurie. When I go inside any store, I have to check all my bags at the door. I hate doing that. Anybody could go through my things."

"Why don't you just leave your things in your apartment?" I couldn't understand why he always carried around so much anyway, now that I knew he had a place to live.

"Same thing. Someone could get in my apartment. The lock on the door is broken anyway." He paused and then added, "Well, I'll just have to leave some of these things there and take a chance. As long as I keep my important papers with me, it should be okay."

I thought about J.C.'s paranoia about people wanting to take his belongings and knew that something simple like going into a store was stressful for him. He didn't feel safe unless he had his belongings with him at all times. I remembered when he needed some envelopes and never explained to me why he didn't just go buy them. Now I understood better.

He continued talking about the apartment. "I'm convinced that this place is bugged. I hear voices all the time while I'm in there, people saying things like, 'There he is, I wonder where he's been all day,' or 'He's getting up early today.' I don't feel safe there."

I felt sorry for J.C.--he distrusted others so much, that he felt like he always had to be on guard. I wanted to gently confront him on this but knew he couldn't be swayed.

I told him that he should start looking for a new place, and I would help him with the security deposit. I questioned his money management skills--what happened to your Social Security check that I cashed for you last week? He said he spent it on food, laundry, paid off $200 debt. I told him I was concerned how he went through money so fast.

"Do you have some kind of budget, J.C.?"

He looked at me strangely, and I realized that a budget for a homeless person did seem kind of ridiculous. I remembered what Sarah had said about how a homeless person can't deal with budgets. That was part of the life they left behind, and the structure it created was very stressful.

"You have an income, and although it is small, you do need to learn to manage your money," I emphasized.

He nodded in agreement, although I wondered if he was at a place where he could do this. All I could do was make the suggestion.

Bit by bit we were making progress. "You definitely want to get off the street--this is your goal, right?" I looked at him intently and he nodded his head. "Then you need a plan, one that takes in account more than just a day or two." He agreed, and we focused on small steps--getting his picture taken, getting a passport and opening a bank account.

"Once you've accomplished these smaller steps, you will be closer to reaching your goal." J.C. was smart; he knew these things. Yet he had difficulty following through on the things that were best for his overall situation.

My thoughts kept going back to the issue of money. There had to be more to it than the loans J.C. kept referring to. J.C. had mentioned a system he had developed for playing the lottery--one that was mathematical and couldn't fail. Could this be where his money was going? Or was he involved in other kinds of gambling? But no matter how often I persisted in asking him, he always had the same explanation--the loans.

The days were passing by quickly, and it was just a matter of time before J.C. would be on the street again. He said he'd been looking for another apartment but wasn't having any luck. Everything was too expensive--his Social Security check couldn't even begin to cover the rent.

But he didn't get discouraged. He continued to sit on his corner each day and mentioned to others that he was looking for an apartment. This strategy proved to be successful--one of J.C.'s clientele told him about an apartment.

"Someone found a place for me." J.C. knew I had been worried; I had been relentlessly bugging him.

"You did! Really?" I was excited, my eyes lighting up as I waited for him to tell me more. "So tell me the details."

"Now, I almost didn't tell you cause I didn't want to get your hopes up." He also didn't want to get his hopes up, I thought.

"Well?" I looked at him questioningly.

"Well, there's this man who's been one of my regulars for years. I told him about my situation one day, and he said he might be able to help me. He said he had to check a few things out first. I'm meeting him tomorrow to look at an apartment. It sounds good but I want to see it first."

J.C. told me later that the apartment was reasonable, immaculate, and in a desirable location. It wasn't huge but it had a little terrace that overlooked a grassy, tree-lined area.

"He's able to work something out with the landlord so the rent will continue to be rent stabilized. That's the only way I can afford it."

"It sounds too good to be true, J.C." I paused for a moment, my hair blowing into my eyes. "Someone's sure looking out for you, J.C." I shook my head, my eyes holding a hint of bewilderment. "I'm so glad. You can't imagine."

"I want you to see the apartment, Laurie, and see what you think. I want you to meet Guy, also. He's an interesting guy; an educator, also."

He made arrangements with Guy to show me the apartment. He was right--it was a modest, but well-kept apartment in a nice, safe building. I told J.C. that I could see him living there. He had found his home.

Should not the giver be thankful the receiver received?
Is not giving a need? Is not receiving mercy?
Friedrich Wilhelm Nietzsche

18 A Larger Dose

The rain hadn't stopped all morning, but I eventually ventured outside, wearing my "grandma" coat, my hat pulled down over my forehead, and my long scarf wrapped three times around my neck. The cold wind and rain still sent a chill through my body.

It didn't seem like a good day to get together and talk with J.C., but there was something about the pouring rain and dismal gray sky that gave a calming effect to our interview. As it turned out, this effect would be greatly needed today.

"Let's find a place that's under cover," I suggested.

"Let's see. I know a place." We began walking into the park and he'd stop every once in awhile and look around. "Over there," he pointed. We climbed some steps and walked into an open-air type of atrium. The wooden slats formed an awning but the rain dripped down between them on the bench. "This is as good as we'll get," he said.

J.C. didn't want to share my umbrella with me. I held it over my head while he began talking into the tape recorder. Suddenly he stopped talking.

"Laurie, I don't mind if you have an umbrella but look at this!" He pointed to the water dripping off the end of the umbrella onto his hat.

"Oh my gosh, J.C. I'm so sorry." I immediately closed the umbrella. "You know, it's not really helping much anyway," I said, pointing to the pile of water that had accumulated on my lap.

He laughed when he saw that. "We are just two fools, aren't we? Sitting here in the pouring rain. No one could ever say we aren't determined to write this book!"

He was right. This was true dedication.

I knew J.C. had more to tell me, and I couldn't imagine what that would be. I am basically a quiet, unassuming person, but I make sure I delivered my points in a very specific way. I was treating J.C as if he was a child or the student, and I was the parent or the teacher. Although he needed structure and someone to keep him focused and goal-oriented, it was crucial that he made his own decisions so that he would feel empowered.

He seemed humbled when I said, "It all boils down to trust and responsibility, J.C. I have to trust that you will follow through on the things we discuss. And trust is built on honesty. Answer my questions directly. Don't always be so evasive."

I let this sink in for a moment, then asked, "So what is it, J.C.?" My eyes locked on his dark glasses.

His forehead seemed to tighten, and his eyebrows lifted over his glasses. "Well, there is one more thing, actually. This is going to be the real shocker." He seemed to grapple with words, and then looked away for a moment. Taking a deep breath, he began.

"I told you about living in New Bern, graduating with honors, attending college." He paused and took a deep breath. "I left out this part. I got married. Right out of high school. I'm still married, as we speak. My wife, Mamie and me, we have seven kids."

My mouth dropped open, as if I was choking on a piece of food.

"We moved to New York, right at the peak of my career."

I was speechless as he continued talking.

"Billy, Mechell, Bonny, Bobby, Adele, Pamela, and Jeffrey. Four children born in North Carolina; the other three born in Long Island."

My voice returned, but my words were spoken tentatively. I had to say something. "You're married and you have children? Where are they?"

"I don't know. In Long Island, I think. That's where they were when I last saw them."

We had spent so much time together, and he had never mentioned a family. I remember once talking about the special bond I had with Joey, and he had changed the subject quickly. That should have been my first clue, but he hadn't indicated in the slightest way that he had children. I swallowed deeply, not sure if I wanted to hear more. "I don't understand, J.C. What happened?"

"I left them, getting in over our heads in debt, problems in the marriage; I just had to get out of there. I'm not proud of it, but that's what I did. I acted impulsively, not thinking about what I was doing, only to regret it later. We were married right out of high school. Stayed together all that time while I was in the Air Force and in college. When I decided to come to Manhattan, our problems really started. I had that need for adventure in my life. I was used to having a lot of things going on and wanted a new challenge. I just wasn't happy in New Bern."

"Well, J.C., I can understand that. Many people move away from their hometown and settle somewhere else. What did your wife think about it?"

"She didn't want to leave but she was very devoted to me and wanted to support me in my decision. So I came to New York, knowing immediately that I wanted to live here. I got a job in Manhattan, bought a house on Long Island, and moved my family to New York. The children did really well with the move, and the following year I got a teaching job closer to our house. Mamie and I had three more children during those years: Bonny, Pamela, and the youngest, Jeffrey. I told you about the homes we bought and how we were in debt. Teachers were paid better in Manhattan so I went there to find a job."

"I would go home on weekends at first, and then gradually started going home less often. I liked the excitement of the city. But it was much more than that. I liked living alone. I liked coming home to a quiet environment. I didn't feel crazy anymore. I knew I had another life with responsibilities and commitments, but I got caught up in the glimmer and glitz of city life. When I'd go back to see my family, I just knew I didn't fit in anymore. Looking back, I never should have gotten married so young and had a family so soon. It was like I had two lives. In Lindenhurst, there were ball games to go to, homework to help with, and lawns to mow. In the city, there were late-night parties and new people to meet. I liked my independence."

I stood up and looked at J.C. with a serious face. "You left your family. Left them, just like that? That's hard for me to understand." I looked at him very intently, my words icy-tipped, my eyes sharp as glass. "When people have problems, they go to counseling or separate for awhile, but to just get up and leave a wife and seven kids?" My eyebrows gathered tightly across my forehead.

J.C. looked at me with an unusual stare. "I'm not proud of what I did. We argued all the time, mostly about money. You see, I liked having nice things, and I spent too much on the house, on furniture, clothes, and cars. Mamie wouldn't get a job."

"Well, she was probably pretty busy taking care of the kids, J.C." His logic was annoying me. "Why didn't you just stop spending so much?"

"You know, I always had this vision of where I wanted to be--I set my sights high. I wanted to be rich, and even if I couldn't be rich, I lived like I was."

"But you walked out on a situation that was of your own doing!"

"I know. I know." I could tell he was getting frustrated. He didn't want to take ownership of the financial problems. He simply just ran away from a bad situation that he had, in effect, created. I didn't know anything about J.C.'s childhood, except for his accomplishments in sports and academics. His parents were strict, but he didn't lack for attention. Maybe there was too much pressure on him to always be the best and achieve the best. Could this be how overspending begins?

"Well, what about the house?"

"We lost that."

We were quiet for a long moment.

"It wasn't that I stopped loving her, but I couldn't live in that environment." He sighed heavily; his eyes beneath his glasses seemed to fog up as if he had moved into another dimension. "Our house was so crowded. The endless noise and confusion was too much. I couldn't separate the tears from the laughter. I couldn't bear the closeness of bodies, the overlapping voices, demanding and needing. At times I'd leave the house and not come back until late at night, when it was quiet and peaceful and no one was around." J.C.'s voice was low and whispery, and he clasped his hands together. "I was afraid of what I might do if I stayed there. I could feel the tension mounting inside of me like a can of pop that has been shaken too much. I didn't trust myself anymore. Leaving there was all I could do, was the best thing to do."

As J.C. talked, I knew he was very torn, not proud that he couldn't manage a life as a husband and father in direct contrast to how successful he'd been in other areas of his life. He wasn't a malicious person; he was someone who was fragile inside despite his outward polish. The need to be the best--the need for perfection that he imposed on himself and probably carried over to his family. He had set himself up for failure--perfection is the last thing you'd find in a busy household. The disorder and hecticness of his home life must have created an insurmountable amount of stress, culminating in his need to escape.

I paused as his breathing slowed down. "You did what you had to do." A beat of silence passed by. "You didn't get a divorce?"

"No, Mamie wouldn't even consider that--her religion, her wedding vows and so on and so on."

I wondered how she could have remained married to him when he wasn't there in her life anymore. "Did you see your kids?"

"At first I did, but after awhile I went back less frequently. It was too hard to deal with the family, all the guilt I felt while I was there."

"So you just sent child support and alimony?"

Now J.C. stopped talking for a moment. "I did at first but then I stopped. I was immature, irresponsible and selfish; I admit that. I feel terrible about that. I don't know how Mamie ever made ends meet. I know she went back to work, and she also collected welfare. I tried to send money to them, but my lifestyle in the city ended up costing me a lot. I was lucky enough to have money just for myself. Even though I was still teaching, I had to borrow money and learned to run when I couldn't pay it back. I worked a second job, trying to get my debts paid off."

"Didn't you worry about how they'd manage?"

J.C. stopped suddenly. "I ran away from that situation because I couldn't deal with it. I was a coward; I was a jerk. I don't know why, but I just fell apart. In the city, I could forget. I did whatever I could to forget."

"What, J.C.? Drugs? Alcohol? Other women?"

He looked at me with a somber face. "It doesn't matter." He shook his head. "I didn't know what I was doing. But over time, I knew I couldn't keep living like that. Once I make up mind about something, I do it. I don't go back and forth questioning my decision. I quit the party scene and settled down. I guess I had gotten it out of my system. I'd think about Mamie and the kids now, not having seen them for so long."

"I went to work each day and came home and just stayed inside. Sometimes I watched T.V. but mostly I'd just sit and think. My coworkers started to ask me if something was wrong, but I didn't see any reason to be concerned."

"I quit teaching, like I told you. I couldn't do it anymore. I had always loved it, but now I was irritated all the time by the disrespectful way the students acted. I was having some problems with my temper, but there wasn't anything wrong with me except that I didn't want to be bothered by all the nonsense that went on in that school. So I quit without finishing off the year. That was 1975, more than 10 years after I had left my family."

"I went back to Lindenhurst, to Mamie and my kids. I called and said I wanted to try to work things out. And I really did. I went back with the intention of making my life work and wanted to be a responsible father and husband. I interviewed for a teaching position at Lindenhurst High School and got hired to teach math."

"The first few weeks there flew by, and I spent time with my kids trying to get to know them, proud that Mamie had raised them to be respectful and polite children. I entertained them with my magic tricks and my drawings and my stories about the city. They were in awe of me; I didn't deserve this attention, yet I relished in feeling loved and appreciated."

"Did they remember you?"

"Of course they did! Even the youngest, Jeffrey. He didn't know me at all, but he knew I was his father. And Mamie was so happy I was back!"

"Then it happened again. Things had been going well with the family, but soon the ceaseless noise and activity that roared throughout the house started reverberating through me, my insides twisting and turning inside out. Mamie and I ended up arguing a lot, and when she said she didn't want me teaching in Lindenhurst, I blew up. I never said goodbye, just left without a word."

"Why didn't she want you to teach there?" I wondered if something had happened when J.C. taught at Wyandanch High School and Mamie didn't want it to happen again. But what?

"I don't know. I really don't know." J.C. shrugged his shoulders but didn't say more. "I went back to Manhattan and since I had some money saved, I didn't have to look for a job. I found a room to rent in Harlem, and I'd spend my days inside just thinking, mostly sleeping. Sometimes I'd go and sit in the park and watch people walking by. A few friends called to see how I was but eventually they stopped calling, realizing I didn't want to be bothered. I had never felt so down, and I couldn't get myself out of it."

"J.C. You were really depressed. Did you try to get any counseling?"

"No, I don't believe in telling my problems to a complete stranger. Remember, I'm a very private person. Anyway, I still had the car I brought with me from Lindenhurst, and I'd go to Long Island and drive around for hours, usually driving through Lindenhurst and past the street where my family lived. Sometimes I'd just park the car nearby and watch the kids come home from school. I wanted to stop but I didn't know what I'd say and I had nothing left to give them."

"I had to find some work, though, because my money was running low. I started driving a taxi, I figured since I was spending my time driving around anyway, I might as well make some money at it. My spirits improved, and I moved out of the small room I was renting and found an apartment."

"I came up with a plan; it kind of just evolved from all my hours of just sitting and thinking. I needed money. Lots of it cause I wanted to make up for deserting my family, and the only thing I could give them now was money. I worked as a recreation assistant at night and started saving my money. I hid my money; I'd take it out and count it over and over again, and then hide it again. I didn't want to take any chances by putting it in a bank where anyone could steal it. All I thought about was how I could make more money. My funds started growing, slowly but steadily."

"As I told you before, I had some bad luck--the car accident-- and my plan for accumulating money came to a halt. In fact, I had less than before the accident because I had to use my savings to supplement my disability payments."

"When my back was finally healed, I got my job back as a taxi driver and did some freelance photography. My life felt empty, though. I was alone, unable to understand why I couldn't cope with a family life. I just knew I needed a quiet, simple life where I was in complete control. And I couldn't control a life that was full of the complexities of a large family. It had been more than ten years since I had left my family, and I knew that I had made a mistake. My children were growing up without me, and I really missed them. Because of many years of hard feelings, I was estranged from them and had no contact with them. I felt so bad that I wasn't there for them. I lost my home, my wife, and the support of my community. And now look at me, I have nothing." His face looked forlorn and weary, like an old dog roaming the streets. "I'm just an old man with lots of regrets."

"But, J.C. You have a family. Maybe you can try to find them."

"Not now. Not when I'm like this." He thought for a moment. "You know, I was almost there. I was going to surprise them on Thanksgiving Day. I didn't expect them to welcome me back, but I wanted to give them the money I had saved. $35,000. Do you believe it? And then the nightmare began--the drug dealers entered my life."

I identified with his reaction to stress, the feeling of just wanting to run away and hide. But when things were overwhelming for me, I'd take time to process my feelings and then the stress became manageable. But J.C. wasn't able to do this. He tried--he went back to the house to try again. His own defenses and pride prevented him from seeking help, yet this could have been a place to

111

start. Denying his feelings and trying to deal with the situation on his own probably only created more anxiety. In his mind, he could only fill his life with excitement and adventure to mask his underlying pain, but soon he reached the point where he withdrew completely. It was sad that he could feel at ease only at his panhandling corner. It was the only place where he could interact with others without any threat of closeness and remain in control of his situation. The positive strokes he received there satisfied his need for attention and love.

He knew his family could receive welfare as long as he wasn't there. He was taking care of them in the only way he was capable of--as an absent father. He must have really thought they were better off without him. Then to ease his mind, he became obsessed with money as the only solution. If he had enough money and only then, he would return. That was how he'd make amends.

Now that I knew he had a family, I felt like there was a chance for him to reconnect with others. So much depended upon their response to him--would they want to see him again or would their bitterness be too great? More importantly, did J.C. want to see them?

"But you do want to see your family again?"

"Someday. When I have something to give them. I can't do anything for them now. It doesn't matter how needy and desperate I am, I never want to ask them for help, not after deserting them like I did."

"I'm glad you have a family somewhere, J.C. I really am. But I have to tell you, it really bothers me what you did."

"I know. I know."

"Even though you explained it to me, I'm really angry at you right now. All along you kept this from me, as if you were playing a game, stringing me along. I feel betrayed and manipulated. If I can't believe you are really a good person underneath, then it's hard for me to want to keep helping you."

"I don't know what to say, Laurie. I know that leaving my family was a terrible thing. I just couldn't help it. I didn't see any other way at the time. I was a mess. And then too much time went by and it was too late to make it right."

112

"A lot of people were hurt, J.C. It's hard for me to understand how a caring father would choose not to see his kids grow up. You missed their whole lives and they've grown up with a void in their hearts--knowing that they had a father somewhere that just didn't care about them anymore."

J.C. just sat there with his head down, and I felt like a reprimanding parent.

"I just need some more time to think about this, okay? You think about it, too; maybe you can tell me more that will help my understanding of the situation." I got up and started to leave with just a half-smile. "Are you going to be all right?" He nodded, but when I looked at his face, he had removed his glasses and his eyes were no longer clear and vibrant. They looked like pools of mud washing downstream. He shut them tightly and rocked back and forth as I walked away.

If a free society cannot help the many who are poor, it cannot save the few that are rich.

John F. Kennedy

19 Trying to Make Sense

If there was ever a time that I wanted to walk away from this whole thing, it was now. I accepted that J.C. had me followed and found out where I lived because of safety concerns. I accepted that he had an apartment the whole time I thought he was homeless. But I couldn't accept that he abandoned his family.

As I read through the drafts of my writing, I was confused. I had so many questions and just couldn't understand how someone who presented himself as being a good, caring person could have lived his life so contradictory. This book had taken a lot of work, and I was angry that he wasn't totally honest with me at the beginning. Yet, there wasn't anything smug about him; it didn't seem like he was trying to use people.

I thought about how stress affects me and found an entry in one of my journals written some time ago. "I like the quiet. The layers and layers of my life that I have to work through mesh better when I'm surrounded by quiet. Noise tenses my muscles, and when my muscles are tense, my feelings freeze. My skin seems to thicken, and I am unaware of what lies beneath. I can go in and out of this world of mine and take comfort in knowing that my existence isn't totally dependent on the world out there."

As I read that, I thought--does this mean I'm crazy? Did J.C. need this quiet--this space--in order to function? I wanted to know more about him as a person and not just the things he did and didn't do, but how he felt and how he coped with his life.

Why did I believe in J.C.'s goodness and innocence in spite of all that I knew about him? That's where the answer had to be--if I was still convinced of his goodness, then maybe I could understand the emotional turmoil he experienced.

I reflected back to all the hours I had spent talking with him and observing him on his corner. His friendliness and genuine appreciation of others set him apart from other homeless people I had seen. He went out of his way to get ice for the man who had hurt his head. He ran after another man to warn him about a possible robbery. I saw him carry strollers down the steps, catch the arms of people so they wouldn't trip and fall, and give directions to people who were lost. He left his post to console Rob about the loss of his father. He gave money to another homeless person for lunch. He paid special attention to children and had a kind word for every dog. My safety worried him the most. He gave me advice about where to go and where not to go. He told me how to watch my belongings and how to be street smart. He was always concerned about how Joey was doing in school and was concerned if he was safe riding the subway on his own. We had become his family, and he made it his business to make sure we were okay.

He spent hours sitting at his corner completely involved in each passing face. His reason for being there was not just to collect money, but to give something back. And each person who put change in his cup or put a dollar into his hand left with a smile. I saw it happen every day. He chose this as his means to survive. He didn't get involved in drugs or crime. His plan for getting back on his feet might have seemed unrealistic to many, but part of his charm was his optimistic attitude.

I was aware that his "marketing strategies" guided his behavior, but beneath his businesslike sense, there was a joy that emanated from within--it was in his smile, his eyes, and his body posture. It couldn't be faked--it defined him. It was this glow that touched the many people who saw him each day--it attracted me to him. The way he construed his world was a result of his emotional problems. If he was manipulative and irresponsible, it was because he was paranoid and untrusting. If he was controlling, it was because change was unbearable. If he was isolated, it was because he couldn't tolerate closeness. If he was delusional, it was because he didn't perceive reality accurately. If he was curt or abrupt, it was because he was anxious. If he was self-righteous, it was because he couldn't tolerate differences. If he was egotistical, it was because the only world he could manage was his own. If he had a self-inflated ego, it was because it was too devastating to him to admit any weakness. His choices were guided by his need for survival--his life was a result of unresolved emotional issues. He functioned the best way he could, and maybe remaining homeless for so long was how he handled his guilt.

I knew I wanted to write the truth. But did I really need more details about his life or did I just have to reaffirm my belief in his underlying goodness?

I had exhausted all my resources for finding information on J.C.'s life. I had spent a lot of time online, but, I wasn't qualified to do serious investigative work. The only way I could find out about J.C.'s past was to find people who knew him. But why? What was it I wanted to know?

I wanted to understand better what J.C. was like when he was young, both as a child and also as a young husband and father. Perhaps if I had more insight into his psychological past, I could understand better what led him to the decisions he made. The only way I could explain his abandonment of his family now was to surmise that J.C. was suffering from many emotional problems that he was unable to deal with. I didn't feel that he was a malicious person--he was just a troubled individual.

I knew this was a very delicate thing--confronting someone who has problems but doesn't see them. J.C. still thought he was the victim, he was where he was today because of what had happened to him, and not because of the choices he made. The nature of mental illness is to continue to live in a world that is based on nonreality. Maybe if the kids knew more about the illness, they could understand better why he did what he did. He's not a bad person, just a person who never got any help with his problems. He survived the only way he knew without going completely crazy.

What is goodness then? It's that part of a person that is pure and loving and unselfish. It's the open heart; the effortless giving that needs nothing in return. It's the innermost part of our being--the part of us that is most godlike, most selfless. It's the part of us that remains untouched by the rest of the world, that radiates in light and joy and never ceases to be. It's the most evident in the face of a newborn baby or a parent singing his child to sleep. Years of living through pain and hurt build in layers over this goodness inside us and some never find it again. Some find it but only with the help of others. Sometimes our lives are so distorted that the goodness becomes unrecognizable, and although it doesn't cease to exist, it is never seen.

I went back to my gut feeling--J.C. was a good person. This was a person who was not aware of his misperceptions. He honestly felt he had been wronged. He was just beginning to take responsibility for the things he had done in his life that had hurt others and himself. His sincerity rang true--he really believed what he was saying, he didn't see it any other way. He knew he had wronged others but did what he thought he had to do in order to survive--simply that. It was not his intention to hurt others.

Although I was upset because J.C. hadn't been up front with me, I still felt a close bond with him. Knowing this, I decided to try to accept J.C. for the person he was--a goodhearted but confused individual. I would continue to help him in the best way I could--by being his friend and help him become more aware of his emotional issues. I had invested so much time with J.C., I was determined that I would work with him so he could make some progress in finding a home, managing his life, and maybe finding his family.

.

Every problem has a gift for you in its hands.
Richard Bach

20 A Family Lost

Spring was here. The park was more beautiful this time of year, not just because of the new blooms on the trees and bushes, but the scent that traveled with me as I walked along the paths. I thought about what I was going to say to J.C. this morning. I met him at the playground around 11:00.

"Like I said before, J.C., I believe you are a good person deep down. But I think you must have been up against some terrible things, both externally and internally, to have made some of the choices you did. Something happened or maybe it was just a gradual thing, but it has kept you from being successful and sensitive to the needs of others."

He shook nervously like a wobbly table. He bent his head in concentration and finally raised it like a heavy weight.

"I made a mistake. I wish I could undo what I did. But I can't, and all I can do now is feel remorse and pray for forgiveness."

I studied his face for a long time, as if I was looking for a crack in a sheet of ice. Gradually, the lines in his face smoothed into his skin. I cleared my throat, searching for words.

"Maybe I can find out some things about your family, J.C."

He flashed an appreciative smile. "I would really like that. I care about what's happened to them. I just don't want them to know about me."

"Well, I'll see what I can find out. Let me write down the names of your kids and their birth dates." I got a piece of paper out of my bag.

"Now, what if I find out any bad news. You still want to know?"

"I want to know whatever you find out. I want you to tell me."

I got online and started looking for information. Anything about him or his family, any news articles from the Lindenhurst newspaper, something that would help me understand better. I looked up the Social Security Index and was surprised at what I found.

I handed J.C. a piece of paper the next day.

"I think this might be about your wife, J.C. It's not good." My voice was quiet, and my words were spoken tentatively.

He slowly set down his cups and looked at the paper, reading carefully the name, place of birth, and date of birth. His smile slid off his face like melted snow. "This is Mamie." He pointed to the date of death and muttered quietly. "1996. She was only sixty-two years old. I can't believe it." He shook his head slightly, and his lips quivered. "I wonder what happened."

"I'm sorry, J.C."

He stared at the ground and folded the paper in half. His eyes tightened like a stubborn jar lid, and his knees moved like marbles when he stood up. "I never expected that. I always thought there would be time." His head swayed slowly, back and forth, back and forth. He met my eyes to keep from falling.

"I just can't believe it," he said. "She's gone." The air felt heavy around us. "She was such a good person. Perfect, actually." He swallowed slowly, his eyes watered-up. "I didn't appreciate her, that's for sure. And she raised our kids by herself. A strong, a very strong woman."

I stood silently next to him and pat his arm. I thought it might help him if he told me more about her. "What was she like, J.C.?"

"Mamie--she was one of a kind. She was tall, lighter skinned than me, high cheekbones, warm eyes; she was beautiful, inside and out. Stayed devoted to me and always put others first. I know it wasn't easy for her. She worked three jobs after I left." He formed a slight smile. "She would open her heart to everyone. No matter what anyone needed, she gave it to them. She was struggling financially, yet welcomed anyone who needed a meal or a place to stay. She was too good for me, and I always knew that. I didn't deserve her." His voice quieted slightly. "I wanted to go back and make it up to her. And now I can't." He took off his darkened glasses to wipe his eyes.

"I'm so sorry. I shouldn't have told you, J.C." My voice was shaking.

"No, I'm glad you did." He sighed heavily and then spoke tentatively. "I wonder how she died. I hope it wasn't because of me."

"What do you mean?" I didn't understand. What could he have to do with her death?

"I don't know. I'm just sorry she's gone."

"Well, maybe her obituary will indicate the cause of death, if we can locate that."

J.C. nodded. "You know, Mamie being gone now--it changes everything for me. I've lost the chance to make it right. I just never thought . . ."

"But you have your kids," I said.

"I just know they must hate me, and I don't blame them. After what I did."

"It's never too late to go back, apologize, ask for forgiveness. Explain to them what happened. You're the only father they have. You have to try. Don't decide for them." My words were tightly formed, spoken with precision.

"It's just that I took so much for granted, thinking life would go on and on. I can't get back what I've lost, no matter how hard I try."

"You can do something now before it's too late, J.C. Find your kids. You have to." Regrets . . . I thought. Looking back and wanting to transform moments into a different reality, moments indelibly carved inside, surfacing in a tear, a sigh or a sleepy dream. The news about Mamie was hard for him to accept. But maybe it wasn't too late for him to reach his kids.

"I don't know what I'd say to them. I'm afraid of what they'd say to me. If I had money to give them, they might be more open to seeing me."

"I doubt if it's your money that they want. But I'll see if they still live around here. If I locate them, do you want me to contact them and see how they feel?"

"Yeah, yeah, that would be a good way to do it. See if they want to talk to me or see me. But don't tell them I'm here--I don't want them to see me like this. Could you do that for me, Laurie?"

I nodded and thought about where to start. I talked to my husband about it, and he suggested we take the train to Lindenhurst. Maybe some of the kids still lived there. It was worth a try.

> If you are patient in one moment of anger,
> you will escape a hundred days of sorrow.
> *Chinese Proverb*

21 Lindenhurst

This was our first train ride out of the city. We studied the map and watched for the Lindenhurst stop. We decided to find the library first. If we looked through phone books and back issues of the local newspaper, we might find something about the Simmons family.

The train ride took about an hour, and as we got further and further away from Manhattan, the streets looked quieter and grass took the place of tall buildings. The train stopped in Lindenhurst, and the station was empty except for a man in the tollbooth. He gave us directions to the library--it was only a few blocks away.

Lindenhurst was a quaint, quiet town not unlike the towns back in Ohio. We passed a church, a grocery store, an ice cream shop and an old post office as we walked. We found the library easily. The librarian helped us find some local newspapers and brought us a stack of high school yearbooks. I started looking through the newspapers, and T.J. paged through the yearbooks.

"Laurie, look here. I found J.C.'s son!" I was sitting at another table, and my stomach fluttered when I heard T.J.'s words.

"Look, it's Billy."

It was--Billy Simmons, basketball star, graduated in 1963.

I picked up another yearbook, and we eventually found pictures of Mechell, Adele, Bobby and Jeffrey. I had to sit back to take it all in. These were J.C.'s children. They were such nice-looking kids with smiles just like his. There were pictures of them throughout the yearbooks in various sports activities. They looked like average high school students, yet I knew that they grew up not knowing if their father was even still alive. I felt a bond with them--it was as if I was the link between them and their father. I felt very emotional, and my eyes watered up.

An elderly black woman sat next to us at the table. T.J. looked at me and said quietly, "You know how there's a reason for everything--nothing is just a coincidence?" I didn't know what he was referring to. He continued. "What did you notice about Lindenhurst High School?"

"Well, for one, it was a predominantly white high school."

"So, who sits by us, but an elderly black woman. If she's lived in Lindenhurst for any length of time, I bet she knows the Simmons family."

T.J. was right. Her kids went to school with the Simmons' kids. Didn't know the family well but knew that the father wasn't there. The mother was sick--breast cancer and died just a few years back. After her son.

After her son?

The oldest--Billy. Died a few years before she did. They were sick at the same time. I think hospice came to their house. Don't know if the kids still live here, though.

We made copies of the pictures from the yearbook and also found a home address. We walked over to that house, but no one was home. We found a listing for Simmons in the phone book and tried calling, but there was no answer. T.J. and I were very quiet on the train ride home, feeling emotionally and physically exhausted. I was anxious to tell J.C. what I had found out about how Mamie died. I didn't know how he'd handle the news about Billy. But I knew he'd like the pictures of his children. I wanted to find out first if the other children were all right and if they still lived in Lindenhurst. I decided I would try calling that number again when I got home so I'd have more to tell J.C. the next morning.

> How much of human life is lost in waiting!
> *Ralph Waldo Emerson*

22 Family Ties

"I've been in touch with your father," I said hesitantly to the voice on the phone." He wanted me to call. I'm a friend of his. Is this Bonny?"

"Yeah."

"Well, he wants to know how you'd feel if he got in touch with you." I waited for what seemed to be a long time.

"My father, you say. Well, how is he anyway?"

"He's fine, just wants to get in touch with his kids. He hasn't seen you guys for a long time."

"I should say. Let's see, twenty years or so. He sure has missed a lot."

I felt more nervous as I continued talking, sensing the distance in his voice. "Yeah, he has. I'm sure." I paused. "He's homeless now. Has been for quite awhile."

The silence was nerve-racking. Maybe I shouldn't have called. Maybe his children wouldn't want to see him.

"Well, where is he?"

"I can't tell you that now. He just wants to know if he can contact you."

He didn't answer. I spoke with rushed words. "I'll give you my phone number, and if you would like to know more or if any of the others want to talk to me, they can give me a call." I took a deep breath and got off the phone. What was I doing? I felt terrible--even though J.C. wanted me to call his kids, I felt like he should have called them himself.

About an hour later, the phone rang. "This is Adele Simmons. You talked to my brother Bonny about our father."

I explained that I was a friend of J.C.'s and why I was calling. She was very cautious. She wanted to know exactly where he was.

124

The more I tried to explain, the more nervous I got. I had expected a different response--I was hoping they'd be overjoyed to have news about him. But they didn't know me at all--and although I explained why I was calling, perhaps they questioned exactly what role I played in their father's life.

I had a hard time falling asleep. I was upset with myself most of all. I felt like I was intruding in other people's lives—again, wanting to fix things. What business was it of mine? Was I doing this just because I wanted material for the book or was I really trying to reunite J.C. with his children?

I went down to see J.C. the next morning, but he wasn't there. I was glad in a way. Although I had news for him about his children, I didn't know what I'd tell him about Bonny and Adele. And about Billy.

"Call them back, Laurie," my husband said. "Tell them the whole truth. Explain about the book and how you met J.C. Tell them what J.C.'s situation is now and how he isn't ready to see them yet. Let them decide if they want to try to see him."

I knew he was right. I felt like I was being deceptive by not telling them all the details. I felt torn--I didn't want to betray J.C.'s confidence but they wanted to know where they could find him.

I didn't have to call them back. That night Mechell called.

I went into the bedroom and closed the door. I took a deep breath and began to talk. But as soon as Mechell began talking, my nervousness subsided--she was so happy that I had contacted them.

"My father! You can't imagine how long I've prayed for this day! To know that he is alive and well means so much to me."

I opened my heart to Mechell and told her my story, her father's story. She was so concerned about J.C.'s welfare, and of course, she wanted to see him. I explained the best that I could that J.C. wasn't able to see them yet. She accepted it.

"I always remember to push," she added.

"Push?" I questioned.

"Yes. P.U.S.H. Pray until something happens."

Something did happen. And Mechell was elated.

A cheerful heart causes good healing.
Proverbs 17:22

23 A Place to Live

The next morning I went down to see J.C. He was talking to someone, and I waited off to the side until he was alone.

"Well, I got good news, Lady Laurie! I'm moving into the apartment this weekend. The timing couldn't be better." He showed me his eviction notice. "I have to be out by Monday."

"Well, I'm glad you have a place to go," I said. "Now let's talk about moving. Do you have someone to help you?"

"No, not really. I'd have to pay someone, and I don't have the money. So I'll probably just take what I can."

"Look, if you had some money, do you think you could find someone to move your stuff for you?"

"Sure, no problem. People will do anything for money."

"Okay." I hesitated before I gave him money to cover the move. He had a way of making money disappear. "Don't lose it or spend it on anything else, J.C."

"Don't worry. I won't. I can't. I have to get my stuff out this weekend."

I waited there quietly for a moment. "There's something else, J.C."

"You found the kids? Well, tell me. Come on. Is it good news or bad?"

I got out a little scrapbook I had picked up for him and handed it to him. He opened it and saw the yearbook pictures of his children. His smile covered his face, and he nodded as he spoke. "Yep. That's Mechell. Just like I remembered her. And that's Billy and Bobby. I wonder how tall they are. And Adele and Jeffrey. He looks just like his mother. But Pamela and Bonny are missing." J.C. turned the

126

pages and took in each picture as if he were reading a book. "How did you get these, Laurie?"

I explained to him how T.J. and I went to Lindenhurst. I told him about the library, going to see the house, and finally, talking to the kids on the phone.

"You talked to them. All of them?"

"I talked to Bonny, Adele and Mechell. Bonny and Jeffrey still live in the house."

"So how are they?"

"They're fine. J.C. Very happy to hear that you're okay. Especially Mechell." I looked at him intently and then added, "I have some bad news, though. About Billy."

J.C. squeezed his hands tightly and held my eyes. "He has passed. Hasn't he?"

"I'm sorry, J.C. He was sick, died a few years before Mamie."

J.C. was very quiet. "And Mamie?"

"She had cancer, J.C. That's how she died."

I went on to tell J.C. about my conversation with the kids. He wasn't surprised that Bonny and Adele were less enthusiastic. "Adele is like me. She likes to check things out, take her time before she reacts. A lot of common sense. Mechell, on the other hand, shows her emotions more easily."

"Mechell wants to see you, J.C. I didn't know what to tell her."

"I can't see her now. Not while I'm like this. Please try to explain that to her."

"I know, J.C. But you're her father! She's been waiting all these years to find you!"

J.C.'s shoulders started moving up and down, and he stood up and paced back and forth. "I just don't think I'm ready to see them yet. This is going to take time. I need time to process this. After the book is published, then I'll be off this corner, and I'll have something to give them."

I knew that dealing with such an emotional event was going to be difficult for J.C. Somehow, he needed to deal with it on his own, and prepare himself for the emotions that were surfacing.

"Don't worry, J.C. Mechell wants to see you, but she

understands. She's just happy that you are all right."

When I left J.C., I felt confused. I would have thought J.C. would have been anxious to see his children. Yet, knowing him, it made sense that this moment would be extremely difficult for him, and he needed time to get himself ready emotionally. And it went back to his way of making amends--giving his children money. He was hopeful that this book was going to provide the means to do this.

> There was always in me, even when I was very small,
> that I ought to be somewhere else.
>
> *Anna Quindlen*

24 The Youngest

Each of J.C.'s children had unique personalities. I don't know why I thought they'd all react the same way to my news about their father, but each time I talked to a different person, I was surprised how the conversation progressed.

Jeff was very levelheaded and cordial. He called himself the realist in the family. He wanted my help in finding J.C. in the city and wanted to know more specifically where he sat each day. I wanted to tell him but again was torn by my allegiance to J.C.

He talked a lot about J.C. Said he hadn't seen him since he was eleven or twelve years old, but vividly remembered that visit. J.C. had shown him his magic tricks and had drawn pictures for him--one of his mother. He said he didn't know how he felt--if anything, he felt nothing. Wanted to see him but was leery of trusting him. He had adjusted to a life without having a father, and he didn't know if he wanted to open himself up to more hurt. He told me when he would be in Manhattan, and we arranged to meet.

Meeting Jeff was an invigorating experience. He was an energetic, enthusiastic young man. He talked very openly and casually about his family and really had a lot of insight about each of his siblings, as well as his parents.

I decided to level with Jeff. I explained J.C.'s frame of mind and asked him to keep that in mind when he talked to him. I didn't know how J.C. would react--if he would be nervous, irritated, or warm and embracing. Jeff assured me that he would do his best to put J.C. at ease. He didn't have any expectations of a tearful reunion. He just wanted to see him to see if he was all right. I expressed my concern for J.C. not to know of my involvement in this meeting, and Jeff assured me that he wouldn't say anything about me.

129

I knew what morning he was coming in to see J.C. I wish I could have stood nearby unnoticed to see their reunion. Yet it was a private moment--as private as a moment could be on a busy street corner in midtown Manhattan.

Families are about love overcoming emotional torture.
Matt Groening

25 The Beginning of Beginnings

On Monday morning, I stopped by his corner. "So, you got moved?"

He told me Guy had left kitchen items, linens, and stocked the cupboards for him with canned goods. There was even a table, some chairs, and a cot. He was happy that the apartment wasn't completely empty. "Things are going pretty well for me now."

Each morning he returned to his corner, still needing to collect money.

"You're not homeless any more, J.C." I looked at him seriously and continued. "You need a plan. You need to figure out what your next step is." He had to stop panhandling. But panhandling had been his life for so long, could he give it up? Not so much for the donations, but for the people he saw and talked to each day. These people seemed to be his only friends.

"It is hard to believe, isn't it? And I will be ready to stop after the book, after the book . . ." He looked at me with hopeful eyes. "People will want to buy the book, the people I've come to know. That's why I need to stay here on this corner now."

I understood. It did make sense. Others probably had the same questions I had had all this time, and they would want to know his story. And in time, they would know J.C. as well as I knew him.

The next day the humidity of the early morning was already hanging from the air like steam on a bathroom mirror. I saw J.C. on my way to breakfast. Jeff was coming today. I didn't let on that I knew, but I promised J.C. I'd stop by later and bring him some food.

When I got back, J.C. was just starting to pack up his things. "Sure is a hot one, huh, J.C?"

"Yep. That's why I'm finishing up early today. Can't stand this heat anymore."

We talked for a few minutes, and I watched J.C. pack up his things in his organized, carefully thought-out way. As I was getting ready to leave, I was disappointed he hadn't mentioned Jeff. But I didn't want to ask; I didn't want him to know that I had anything to do with it. But J.C. blurted out in a quiet, yet somewhat rushed voice. "Jeff stopped by this morning."

"Jeff?" I tried to act surprised.

"Yeah, early. Around 7 a.m. I was just getting set up and situated. He walked up and said hello, stood by me as I sat down. He said a few things, then asked if I knew who he was."

"I said that I did. In less than 60 seconds, I knew it was Jeff, especially after he mentioned a family member." J.C. stopped for a minute and moved his shoulders up and down, like he does when he's excited or nervous.

"He's a tall, nice-looking young man--bright eyes and friendly smile. I saw his mother in his face, the high cheekbones. He asked me to stand up to see how tall I was, then asked me to take off my sunglasses so he could see my eyes. Right then I knew there was no mistake. This was my son, and he was smart, real smart. No sunglasses to hide behind, he wanted to see the real me."

"So it was Jeff! How exciting, J.C. I'm so happy for you!"

"Yeah, my son. And I was impressed, really impressed with how he handled himself. Didn't ask me a lot of questions, I could tell that he was checking out my reactions carefully, really wanted to make sure I was comfortable with him being there." He paused for a moment, a slight smile forming on his face. "Very handsome young man, articulate and intelligent." He grinned. "Takes after his father! I think he was surprised at how I looked, as if he were expecting to see a bent-over crippled old man!"

"He gave me his phone number and said I could call or stop by the house any time. Said he and Bonny lived at the house now, but he didn't talk anymore about family, other than mentioning that my grandson, Mechell's son, had recently died." J.C. paused for a moment. "I couldn't believe that. He had his whole future ahead of him. Poor Mechell." He continued talking. "I told Jeff I was working on a special project that should bring me some money and that I'd be in touch after that. He didn't push, just was very smooth, very polished--really tried hard to put me at ease."

J.C. continued to tell me what Jeff said, that none of the others would be by, although he knew Mechell was especially anxious to see him.

"Did he stay long?"

"No, not long but came back later with a camera to get some pictures of me and pictures of the two of us together. I wouldn't be surprised if he comes back again now that he saw that I was okay with seeing him, probably will want to show me the pictures when they're developed." He took a deep breath. "It was good. It was good. I was very pleasant and cordial. I just hope this book makes some money."

"You know that's not what matters to them, J.C."

"But it matters to me. Anyway, he said that he just wanted to see me, and make sure I was okay, and to let me know that there was still love for me back home."

J.C. was very quiet then, and I knew that this was a difficult moment for him. I tried reading his face and realized that he had learned to detach himself from his feelings probably long ago, and looked at things practically rather than emotionally. But as he pressed his lips together, I could see, even through his dark sunglasses, the spark of something in his eyes, something I hadn't seen before. It was like now he was connected to someone, and there was that promise of hope that maybe things really would be different, that it wasn't too late. He saw Jeff, and Jeff still cared.

> We cease loving ourselves if no one loves us.
> *Germaine de Stael*

26 The Last Goodbye

It had almost been a year since I first met J.C. The time flew by so fast and now my husband and I were making our plans to return to Ohio. I had mentioned several times to J.C when I was leaving so he'd have time to get used to the idea. James Greer and I had talked about having a kind of last get-together with J.C. before I left for Ohio. We were J.C.'s best friends now, at least in terms of our commitment to help him get back on his feet. I suggested going somewhere for breakfast; J.C. said he'd prefer the park. That's where he's most comfortable, I thought, open space and fresh air.

We had some soda and snacks and had a nice, leisurely conversation. I reminded J.C. that I wanted him to leave a block of time open for me the next day. That would be our last time together. He said, "Of course. I wouldn't have it any other way, Lady Laurie."

The next morning. I wrote in my journal. "Today I said goodbye to J.C." I didn't know how J.C. would feel, but I sensed that this would be a sad time for him. And for me.

For many months now, we had spent hours and hours talking and got to know each other well, like friends who'd laughed at each other's idiosyncrasies. He knew I tended to be oblivious of my surroundings and walked around like a trusting child. I knew he didn't miss a thing and planned every step he took. He knew I wasn't afraid to argue with him, and I knew he always had to have the last word. A friendship formed on a street corner in midtown Manhattan--a friendship that developed on benches in the park. We were working on a book together but I became his confidant, the only person he felt he could trust his life story with. He selectively told me about his life, but he also owned up to the fact that he was leaving some things out. He told me once, "There are some things, Laurie, that are best not knowing."

We sat on a bench in a small rose garden area outside of an old apartment building. We discussed the book and my plan to come back to New York in a month or so.

"I have something for you, J.C." I gave him a piece of paper that listed all the things we had accomplished this past year.

"Very interesting. Very interesting." He glanced over the list and then chuckled. "You certainly are efficient, Miss Laurie. I like this. I really like this. You never cease to amaze me!"

There were two columns: the first column listed the things we had accomplished such as getting his birth certificate and passport, and moving into a new apartment. The second column was a "to do" list: open bank account, arrange for direct deposit of social security check into bank account, type resume, and so on.

"So you still have a lot of work to do, don't you?" I smiled at him.

He smiled. "Yes, I certainly do." He glanced down at the paper and his smile became wider. "I like this part." He pointed to the paper. "Who is your best friend?" and the typed response, "Laurie, of course."

"It's true, you know. You know me better than anyone." He paused for a moment. "You know, Laurie, I feel closer to you than I have ever felt with anyone for a long, long time, even my family cause I wasn't there to see them everyday. You and your husband and Joey are like family to me."

There were a lot of quiet moments. I said I needed to go--I had some packing to do.

"I'm not crying outside, Laurie, but there's tears inside me."

I said, "I want to give you a hug," and stood up and hugged him. He was dear to me; I was sad to leave him. We walked out to the sidewalk, and I grasped his hand and squeezed it.

"Take care of yourself, J.C."

"Don't worry, I will. My love to your family."

"Love to you also, J.C."

I smiled at him and walked away, glancing back and seeing his wide grin, nodding head, and his hand held up in a wave. I carry that image of him in my heart.

> Everything you do, do it out of sincerity,
> or the benefit of the action is lost.
> *Conversation with God, Book 3*

27 Time Away

Coming home was so exhilarating! Our home seemed like a mansion compared to the small apartment we had been living in. I never appreciated having so much space before. I would no longer take for granted the soothing motion of our glider on the front porch, the deck encased by overgrown trees, or the peaceful mornings with the murmur of birds in the trees. The best part about being home was having my dogs back again--they seemed to always be under my feet, and I knew they had missed me a lot.

After unpacking and settling into our household routine, I got involved in my writing again. I had talked to one of my friends about my book and had given her a copy of the first few chapters. I was anxious to talk to her about it. I realized that a writer, no matter how excited or good she feels about her work, needs to have feedback from others. I was open to any feedback whatsoever--I wanted my writing to be the best it could be.

It's good to have a friend who is honest, who spares no words in delivering a message. That was Barbara. Although she was complimentary about my writing style and language usage, she had problems with the content. I would have preferred that it be the other way around.

I met with Barbara about a week after I was back, knowing from our phone conversation that I would need to stay centered and open to constructive criticism.

She began in earnest. "The story isn't credible, Laurie. I think J.C. has you fooled. All the signs are there--think about it."

"I don't know, Barbara. I still have a strong feeling that he is a good person deep down."

"Why?"

"It's just a gut feeling--call it intuition."

"Do you see the facts, though?"

"Well, I've questioned him on a lot of things. There's a reason why he's not telling me everything. I hoped that he would, but it hasn't worked out that way."

She continued. "Well, look at what he's told you. He's homeless, yet he's employable and extremely intelligent. So, why is he still on the streets? Next, he left his family, looking for fun and adventure. Not too commendable, I'd say. Money slips through his hands--where does it go? I question his explanation about paying back loans for staying at people's houses. Does the money go for drugs, alcohol, sex, or gambling, either past or present? Do you see what I'm saying, Laurie? And in spite of all this unfavorable information, you still maintain that he's worthy of your help. It just doesn't make sense to me."

I felt myself getting angry. She didn't know him. She didn't see how personable and caring he was with people. Yet Barbara had a point--I just couldn't keep explaining away all the unsettling things J.C. had told me about himself. There just had to be a reason why he made these choices. "Maybe something terrible happened to him--like having a nervous breakdown or something--or maybe he did something that he had to cover up."

"Well, Laurie, if he won't tell you, then you'll have to find out so the book will be believable."

I did think something must have happened that influenced his decisions. I did not believe that he was just a con man. I knew for certain he was a man of character who made a mistake. With this in mind, I decided to figure out how I could find out the rest of the story.

I wrote J.C. a letter. It was harsh, but I needed to vent my frustrations.

July 9

Hi J.C.

As I read through my manuscript, I find myself responding in various ways and want to share that with you.

First of all, although I include conversations or events that may portray you in an unfavorable way, I still do believe in your goodness. You have your reasons for making the choices you did during your life, and I have somewhat of an understanding of that. But it is what I am struggling with now.

Please be confident that it is still my intention to complete the book and publish it. But I think it is going to take more time than I had originally planned.

I need to know more about you and what was going through your mind when you left your wife and kids. Did you intend to have such a large family? I don't understand why you got so far in debt when you, of all people--a mathematician--should have known better. What motivated you to keep purchasing homes, cars, and other nice things if financially you weren't able to afford it (I'm familiar with teachers' salaries)? Why was it so important for you to fill your life with material possessions?

Your story is one of bad luck, yet you actually had good luck. You were a star athlete and scholar and you had a winning personality. You were handsome (I take your word on that!) and liked and respected by many. Your wife loved you and was relentlessly devoted to you. You were very successful professionally. You were destined to succeed. Yet, you didn't! You abandoned your family, and chose a life of fun and excitement over them! Your bad luck started when the drug dealers took your apartment, but even then, you could have made different choices to prevent you from being homeless for so long. The resources are out there--I know from talking to some agencies--and you could have found a job with or without their help.

Somewhere, somehow, you lost your drive and your work ethic.

You were brought up in a family that strongly valued hard work and education, yet you abandoned these.

I've been thinking of some possible explanations: 1) you got heavily involved in drugs and/or alcohol that led to your lack of initiative and responsibility; 2) you suffered some kind of emotional breakdown or had emotional problems and you didn't get help; 3) you were involved in some type of crime or illegal activity, such as drugs, robbery, abuse, or gambling; 4) you were involved in other relationships and you didn't want anyone to know; or 5) any combination of the above.

All of this is surmise on my part. But I am a well-learned and perceptive person and feel like I have a good understanding of people. If none of these can explain what happened, then I just need to keep searching until I find out. I really feel committed to write the truth and not just guess at it.

It's hard for me to understand how a caring father would choose not to see his kids grow up. And your kids are amazing! You have a chance now to get to know them as adults and share the love you have for them. They don't want anything from you; they don't want money from the book---they just want you! Think about it. They want to have a father, a grandfather for their kids. They want to be able to share birthdays and holidays with you, Sunday dinners and church. I'm sure they are struggling with their feelings, but it's amazing how open and forgiving they are. It's all in your hands now.

You are a brilliant and charming person. You have so much going for you--do something for yourself now that will make a difference in your quality of life.

You have to do your part, J.C. I have my own ideas of what that entails, but you are the one who must figure that out. And you know I'll support whatever you decide.

I really hope you are doing okay, and I miss talking to you. Take care.

LA

After I mailed the letter, I knew I had made a mistake. I was someone he trusted and cared about, and the letter sounded like I had turned against him. I tried to call him, but he didn't answer, so I sent another letter explaining that although I wanted to know more of the truth, I was more concerned about his welfare. No matter what he decided to tell me or not tell me, I knew that I did not want to hurt him.

> We cannot do great things;
> we can only do small things with great love.
> *Mother Teresa*

28 Back to New York

I was excited to return to New York. I missed the city; I missed walking through the park, browsing through shops, eating at the open cafes and of course, I missed J.C. There were a lot of things I wanted to do while I was there. I was meeting some of his kids in Lindenhurst and looked forward to that. But most importantly, I wanted to spend time with him. I needed to resolve some of the questions I had.

I went back to my favorite place to sit in Central Park. The bench sits on the path that leads into the park, down under a small bridge--kind of an underpass and leads to the playground. This is where I first saw J.C. away from his corner, the time he was coming from the restroom at the playground. It was the first time I felt the knot of fear inside me about my relationship with him.

He was supposed to meet me there at 1:00. I watched and looked around carefully; he taught me well, I thought, always be observant. I felt like he might sneak up and surprise me--that would be his way.

I waited and waited. Each minute could be counted by the beads of sweat building on my forehead. Waiting--my frustration that seemed to rise out of me in a physical form. Where was he? Why wasn't he showing up? I don't know when I finally realized he wasn't coming. My own obsessiveness took over--he's mad, he's hurt, he's sick, he doesn't want to see me anymore. Could it be that the letter I sent him was too harsh and confrontive? Maybe he just decided that the book wasn't going to work after all, not if I was so insistent on pursuing the truth.

You taught me well, J.C., I thought again. It was you who

insisted that I not take things at face value, that I should always be inquisitive and persistent until I was satisfied with the answers. That's what I was doing now--I wouldn't let up on him until he answered my questions.

I went back to my friend's apartment and tried calling him. No answer. I knew I'd go to his corner in the morning. I had to check out the situation. I had to see if things had changed. I could imagine his words--"The thing is, Laurie, I just don't trust you anymore." Even if he decided he didn't want to work on the book, I still wanted to convey an apology for hurting his feelings.

But early Monday morning I saw the cups. He was there, as always. I walked up quietly and extended my hand. "Hi J.C."

He smiled. "You're here."

"You're mad at me, aren't you? I'm sorry if I hurt your feelings."

He stared at me for a moment, looking confused. "I didn't know if you were going to be here yesterday or today. You wrote August 2 in your letter which is today, but said you'd be here Sunday."

"I wrote the wrong date, I guess." I looked at him keenly. "Is that why you didn't meet me yesterday, J.C.?"

He looked at me with raised eyebrows. "Yeah, I thought you were coming today."

"I know. I know. I messed up." I laughed, realizing that I had done it again. I always seemed to make these little blunders--overlooking the details and here was another example of it.

He nodded his head in agreement but only said, "So welcome back, Lady Laurie."

"So how are you. How's everything?"

"Well, I have lots to tell you, that's for sure."

"It's nice to be back. I've missed the city a lot."

He paused and said quietly. "You've been missed. Not a day went by that I didn't think of you."

I smiled and realized how important I was to him. "You know, J.C. We're going to spend a lot of time together this week. Lots of time talking."

"Good, good. I'd like that, Laurie. My time is your time. All I do anyway is sit here and go home to sleep. I'm looking forward to spending time with you, Lady Laurie." He looked at me with keen eyes, waiting for me to continue.

I hesitated but wanted to know. "You got my letters?"

He nodded. "That first letter, that was the greatest letter I ever received!"

I was puzzled--the greatest letter? I wasn't expecting that kind of response. "What do you mean, J.C.?"

"It was written perfectly--the way it was composed. You made your points, but you did it in a caring way. I respect you for that. I really respect you."

"Are you mad at me about the things I said?"

"Of course not. They needed to be said."

"And . . . . Your response?"

"No response, Laurie. You have to come to your own conclusions, just like the many who will read this book."

I was so surprised--he accepted what I had said in such a calm manner. He wasn't denying anything, but he wasn't admitting anything either. "And my second letter?"

"Yeah, got that one, too. You didn't have to apologize. I wasn't mad at you."

I had to take some time to process his reaction to the letters. I never had expected him to take it so lightly--as if he had been waiting for me to finally confront him. And even though I had confronted him, I questioned if it would really do any good. I knew I had to bring it up again and try to get him to open up to me.

I told him I had to leave--I had a doctor's appointment that morning, but I would back the next morning. I grasped his hand-- "It's so good to see you, J.C. I'll be back tomorrow."

Reverence is the experience of accepting that all in life,
in and of itself,
is of value.
Seat of the Soul

29 Lindenhurst, Revisited

I went out to Long Island to meet with Jeff and Mechell. We planned this meeting while I was in Ohio--Jeff had said that Mechell really wanted to meet me. I told him that I'd love to come out to Lindenhurst when I was in New York.

I didn't tell J.C., though. He seemed to have mixed feelings about me seeing them. Maybe he thought they'd influence me in my writing. But knowing them was helping me know J.C. better. Even though they were very young when he left, they still had a sense of him, and he was their father.

It felt so strange going inside their house, the house in which they were raised. Not the same house that J.C. lived in, but his presence was felt there. After all, his picture was on top of the TV, next to their mother's picture. A familiar cozy old-house smell helped me relax and settle into my time with them.

Mechell was beautiful--she shined inside and out. She had suffered many losses in her life, yet her faith kept her strong and positive. Her six-year old daughter, Tamika, was the epitome of beauty--J.C. would be so proud of his granddaughter. She clung to me like a magnet--"You found my mommy's daddy," she said.

I felt comfortable sitting with them as they talked and laughed about the pictures they dug up from a stack of photo albums. Pictures of birthdays, holidays, graduations, and family reunions. Pictures of Billy, Jason, Uncle Tom and a picture of the house J.C. grew up in. Many of their mother--mom at church, mom in the kitchen, mom at their sides. Always there, next to their bright-faced smiles and tiny shoulders.

144

"Is this hard for you?" I asked, thinking that looking at pictures of their mother would bring back the sadness of her death. I didn't even know her, yet my eyes were stinging slightly as if I did.

"No," they said. "We only have good memories of her. This just brings them back."

There was only one picture of J.C. The one on the TV, taken probably when he was in his twenties. I swallowed hard, realizing the absence of him in the hundreds of pictures that passed before my eyes. How sad, what a loss, I thought, that he missed all of this. The smiling and silly faces of his kids, the birthdays and graduations celebrated, and not being able to watch his wife age so gracefully and his children mature. Why? For what purpose? I wanted to go back and shake him hard and plead with him to go back now--it's still there, the love and bond of your family, J.C. Look at these faces, feel their life and joy, in spite of growing up without you. You have more in common with them than you think--they are survivors, just like you.

"What do you hope for?" I asked them.

"For our father to come back and be a part of our family," Mechell said.

Jeff looked at Mechell momentarily and then spoke. "Mechell, it's not going to be like that. He wasn't here while we were growing up. He's not going to be here now. People don't change just like that. Don't set your hopes too high." I remembered that Jeff was the realist of the family. "You know, sometimes it's just impossible to understand why people do the things they do. All we can do is just accept where they are. Our father said he had business to take care of and then he'd be in touch. But I know that after this business, there would probably be something else and then something else. That's okay, though. I just wanted to see that he was doing well and let him know I was there if he needed me."

Mechell nodded, but she seemed disappointed. "It's going to be hard to accept that, but all that really matters to me is that he is alive!"

"All of this may be too overwhelming for your father. Don't forget he's lived alone all these years." I added.

145

"It's in his hands," Jeff continued. "We'll keep visiting him, though, and maybe eventually he'll want to come out and see us."

"Do you want to know why he left?"

Mechell shook her head. "Not really. It won't change anything. Whatever he did and why he did it isn't important. He's my father, and I love him for that reason alone."

"What about you, Jeff?"

"No. I guess I feel the same as Mechell. I just think he set his hopes too high. That's what happens. You keep trying and trying but get nowhere and eventually you lose your motivation. You set your goals high, but each time you find yourself against another wall and it tears away at your drive. So you just start to accept that this is how it is."

I listened to Jeff intently, thinking that he wasn't just talking about J.C.

"This is very typical of what happens to a black man. We have the same obstacles as everyone else, but then we get down to the one thing that can't be changed--our color--and no matter what 'progress' has been made in our society, being black is still a disadvantage."

"You think that's what happened to your father?"

"Maybe. Look how he just kept going further down and down-- from being a teacher and then eventually settling for just being homeless. I don't know--it's more complicated than that. But I don't feel the need to know why he did the things he did."

I watched Mechell and Jeff as they laughed and shared stories about their childhood and noted the differences among their siblings. "Each one of us has a unique way of interacting with others-- Bonny's very quiet, Adele and Pamela are outspoken, and I am the mediator," Jeff mentioned. "Mechell is very agreeable until something upsets her, and then she just lets it all go. But I understand that she's motivated by love and if she's upset, it's because someone hasn't responded to that love."

I looked at Mechell and smiled. "That's a really nice compliment from your brother," I said, realizing again, Jeff's perceptiveness.

"J.C.'s birthday is this week," I said, and they both nodded. "I know." Jeff said. "Tell him I'll be there on Monday morning, okay?"

"I have something for him," said Mechell, "and Bobby also has something." She gave me two cards--one from her and one from Tamika. She pulled out a large envelope from Bobby. "Look at this."

It was an old plaque from the Air Force, with J.C.'s name on it and when he enlisted. "Wow," I said as I studied it carefully. "This will really mean a lot to J.C."

Jeff brought me back to the city that night, and I felt exhausted and exhilarated at the same time. The close bond I felt connected me even more to J.C. This was his family, and the love in their hearts joined them together.

The true meaning of life is to plant trees,
under whose shade you do not expect to sit.
Nelson Henderson

30 J.C. and Me

Today was J.C.'s birthday. Sixty-eight years old! I had a feeling he'd be on his corner today since it was his birthday. I got there early and was glad when I saw his cups.

"Happy Birthday, J.C."

"Thank you kindly, L.A. It's good to see you."

I talked to him for awhile and gave him a few things I had picked up for him for his birthday.

"This is unbelievable. Absolutely unbelievable," he said when he pulled out the small camera and film. He continued pulling items out of the bag and laughed when he saw the stamped envelopes addressed to me. "Is this a hint or something, Lady Laurie?" He chuckled, and he beamed proudly. "I certainly have missed you!"

I watched others come up and wish him a happy birthday. I finally got to meet his friend, Donald, although I had to elbow J.C. to introduce me to him. "Now, J.C. There you go again keeping all the ladies to yourself," Donald kidded.

James Greer came by next, and his smile fit the occasion. I felt like this was a reunion of some sorts. J.C. eased back into the wall as people sent wishes his way. He looked extremely content.

I had gone to his corner a couple of times already this week and was surprised when he wasn't there. He hadn't waited for me like he had in the past. Something seemed different. I knew he still cared about me, but it just seemed like he was less friendly.

"Let's talk today when you're done here," I suggested. We picked a place, and before I left, I gave him the cards from Mechell and Tamika.

"You've seen them this week?" he asked.

"Yeah, I have. I'll tell you more about it later."

I met him at the "rose garden" where we had talked before. He pulled out a bag with the cards he had received today. The first one he opened was from Tamika.

"Well, look at this. Look at this." He read the words quietly. "That's me, her granddaddy!" He pulled out an item from inside the envelope. It was a blue pen attached to a string that he put over his head. The pen had writing on it--it said, "Remember to P.U.S.H." He thought for a moment and then smiled. "That's what Mechell said to me, what you told me about. Pray until something happens. And look, here it is on this pen." He smiled and held the pen in his hand. "I like this. I really like this. This is really something."

Next he opened Mechell's card. He pointed to the words as he read them, noting those that were underlined. Then he read her message aloud. "This is really important. This part--'I want you to know I'll always be there for you, until the end'--that means a lot to me." He closed the card and looked at me. "She must still really love her daddy! She's something else!"

I handed him a large brown bag and said, "This is from Bobby."

"What's this? Pictures?" Then he looked closer and saw the old wooden frame sticking out. "I know what this is. I know what this is." He pulled it out and sat back and held the Air Force plaque in front of him. "Well, I'll be. I never thought I'd see this again. So Bobby had it. Bobby had it. Can't believe it!"

I watched as he read it carefully and pointed to his name. "Here it is. James Clinton Simmons, 1951. That's when I enlisted. But I wonder why Bobby wanted to give this to me?"

"Oh, J.C. He probably knew it would mean a lot to you. That's why."

"Yes, I know. But something else. Something else." He thought for a moment. "He really wants me to get in touch with him, that's it. He knew that if he gave me this, I might decide to call him."

"Well, why don't you? You know he's waiting for you to call."

"I just might. I just might. He's a very wise person, that's for sure." I hoped he would call Bobby. Although Jeff and Mechell had come to see J.C., Bobby was different in that he wanted to know for sure that J.C. wanted to see him. He was waiting for him to call.

"Well, this has been some birthday, Laurie. I can't remember when I had a nicer one!" He held all his things on his lap and then looked at me. "So you went out there this week?"

"Yeah, I did. Jeff picked me up at the train station and we went back to the house. Mechell and Tamika were there. They're beautiful people, J.C. And the house was warm and comfortable--very homey! I liked being there."

"Did you see any of the others?"

"No, just Jeff and Mechell. We looked at lots of old pictures and then went out to dinner. Mechell drove me past the old house and Wyandanch High School. That house really was nice!" I thought for a moment and then added quietly, "Jeff and Mechell are very close to each other. And you'll love Tamika. She's an exceptionally brilliant child! Now, you don't mind that I went out there, do you?"

"No, not at all. In fact, I'm glad you did. You saw the house; you saw that they're all right. That means a lot to me." He put the cards back into a plastic bag and lay them carefully into his backpack. "Family is very important to you, Laurie, isn't it?"

"Yes, it is, J.C. Very much so." I waited just a few seconds and added, "Seems important to you now, too."

He smoothed his shirt and nodded his head. "Sometimes it takes a long time to learn what really matters."

"Do you think you'll ever go out there, J.C.?"

"Yeah, I do. Not for awhile, but soon, I'll visit them.

"They still need you, J.C."

"They do--don't they? It's good to know that. I just hope I don't disappoint them."

We continued talking about his family, and then he stopped and held my eyes with a questioning look.

"There's a few things I want to talk about. I'm going to worry about you while you're here in New York again, Laurie."

"Now, J.C. I'll be fine. But you never do stop worrying about my safety, do you?"

"No, I don't, L.A. I feel responsible while you are here."

150

I knew he did, and I smiled at him. "Tell you what I'll do. I'll call you in the evening, to let you know that I'm home safely."

"That would ease my mind a lot, Laurie. I'd sure appreciate that."

"So how are you feeling, J.C.?" As he gave me an update on his apartment and some of the things he was worried about, our conversation seemed like old times. Nothing seemed to have changed. Even his major problem--he needed money for his loans.

"You know, J.C. About these loans. Explain them to me again."

His story didn't change--he owed money for all the nights he had stayed at these different places over the years.

I told him I thought of a scenario of what might have happened to him years ago. "J.C., I think you made a big mistake a long time ago and because of it, you had to run away. You had to leave your family--you didn't have any choice. It just tore you apart to have to do that to your family. Although you and your wife had problems, you still loved her and you loved your children."

"You know, I left for the reasons I told you before. I had to go to Manhattan to make more money. I intended to go back but it didn't work out that way."

Yet, for him not to keep in touch with his kids--that still puzzled me. I watched his face closely, waiting for him to say more. He closed his eyes, and I continued talking. "J.C., whether you tell me anything else or not, I will publish the book and only suggest what I think happened. No one will know for sure--only you."

This was true. I remembered what Jeff had said about not being able to understand some people and what motivated them to do the things they did. It was time for me to stop trying to understand J.C. and just accept him as he was. I hoped that someday, though, he would tell me more.

Now is the hour that you must go ... .
Bing Crosby

31 There is a Time

There is a time when one has to decide to move on, to find peace in the acceptance of what is. That's how I felt about J.C. It was time to write the final chapter. Not that I wasn't going to see J.C. any more--I knew I'd keep in touch with him and his family and visit him when I came back to New York. But it was time to let go of all the questions, all the seeking and searching. There are some puzzles that have just too many pieces, and I knew I'd never find the missing ones in this one.

My understanding of J.C.'s situation was greatly influenced by the mesmerizing effect he had on me. It was hard for me to be objective, although I kept going back to the facts. Everything he told me he believed was the truth. Over time, people can forget the actual reality of a situation and J.C. needed to believe that things happened the way he said they did.

I've tried so hard to take myself out of my world and put myself in his. It was difficult to refrain from judging him and hold back my own thoughts, opinions, and values. But the times that I'd been able to make that connection to him by saying, "You seem really upset now," or "You must not sleep at night worrying about this," I noticed his shoulders relax, his breathing quiet, and his speech slow down. He stopped looking around himself so often and was able to enter into a real conversation with me.

I couldn't force him to deal with something if he wasn't able to. He was extremely well-defended and had construed his world so he could manage his life. He wasn't able to realize that it was because of his decisions that he continued to live in fear and distrust. Something very simple, like if you paid your rent, you wouldn't have people constantly bothering you. If you answered the phone occasionally, people would stop calling you every day--didn't sink in for him. He was used to viewing life as a constant challenge, and he needed that stimulation to survive.

My final understanding of J.C.'s life is vague and uncertain. He probably did get involved in something that jeopardized his safety and his financial security. I think he is still dealing with this on some level or he wouldn't be so optimistic about this book solving his problems now. But the beauty of our relationship was not just working on the book together. The genuineness of our friendship would never cease to exist, and we both knew that. We were two people from two different worlds, although we both started in the same place. We were both raised in large families, received a good education, became successful teachers and married and had a family. But although his life went in a different direction, we had a bond that was pure and simple. We recognized the goodness in each other.

The story I did get from J.C., although incomplete, was more than just words. His story was about the resiliency of the human spirit and mind when faced with difficulties. It was about human weakness and pain and the importance of forgiving ourselves for our imperfections. And mostly, it was about the goodness that lies deep inside us, even when our clothes are tattered and our emotions are troubled. That goodness, that pure state of unselfish love, is the cord that holds us all together. I found it in J.C.--and he found it in me.

Fear thou not; for I am with thee;
Be not dismayed; for I am thy God;
I will strengthen thee;
yea, I will help thee, and not cast thee away.
(Isaiah 41:10)

32 A Word from the Sponsor

Laurie wouldn't let me forget about a plan. She said that was the best way that I could help my kids. They were worried about me.

"It's time to get a job, J.C. Work on a resume, J.C. I'll help you, I'll type it up for you." So I worked on a resume, trying to recollect the many jobs I had held over the course of my life, focusing mainly on my teaching career.

Resume:

1960-61	Russell Grove High School (Virginia)
1961-62	Staunton High School (Virginia)
1962-63	Massopequa Junior High School
1963-64	Wyandanch Memorial High School
1964-65	Parkway Preparatory School (Queens)
1966-67	Alfred E. Smith Boys School (Bronx)
1967-68	Joan of Arc Junior High School
1968-71	High School of Fashion Industry
1975-76	Booker T. Washington Junior High

I added my other work experience to my resume--medical examiner, corrections officer, insurance salesman, taxi driver, and recreation assistant. I had to admit, it looked pretty impressive! It was a place to start--I studied the classified ads in the newspaper. I also mentioned to many of my regulars that I was looking for a job. Maybe I'd even take my test over for my driver's license, I thought. I might need that. Who knows, maybe I'd drive a taxi again!

I'm still looking and waiting now, but I'm optimistic. I've gotten settled in my new apartment, I've bought some new clothes that I can wear when I go on interviews.

It takes awhile to get acclimated to being homeless, from having everything to having nothing. Making the adjustment to not being homeless was going to take some time. It takes a change of mind set, how one looks at things. I had experienced the discomfort, the tedium of my life, my makeshift and dangerous sleeping arrangements, the indifference of people toward me. A part of me seemed to die from living on the streets, but my life was richer now because of it.

I hope to see all my kids again. I still can't believe that I will be able to talk to them and get to know them. I'm sure that God has sent angels my way, making my dream a reality. Whenever I hit rock bottom, something always happened that restored my faith, kept me from giving up. I believe that Mamie was instrumental in this somehow, that even in her afterlife, this continued to be her dream and that maybe she sent Laurie here to me.

People have asked me what I want to do with my life now. I want to make amends to my kids somehow. That's what's most important to me. But also want to give back to the people that have helped me, who never gave up on me. I hope I can do this by helping other homeless individuals, like I was helped. I think a lot about what I've experienced and learned these past years. I never gave up hope. I never gave up belief in myself. I want to share this with others who find themselves living a life of despair, wondering if it'll ever change. I know that each of us can make a difference, if we only try.

A Special Thanks from J.C.

Frank Bernarvucci
M.J. Kramer
Steve Chamer
Martin Fisher
Jon Ladja
Cornelia Veriotti
Lynore Spencer
Lady Caryn
Deanna
Jim Murphy
Geraldine
Lady Gail
Wendy
Zorith Marshall
Vernon
Clara
Lisa Manley
Karen F.
Eric and wife
Bernard
Mr. Umberto
Libbe
Herbert
Lou Aricson Jr.
Lauren Zio
Tracy, B.
Krzystof
Urszulu
Patricia Leristis
Officer Stemmle, Jim
Jake Anderson

Chris Thomas
Tecla
Phil Miller
Vanessa
Cindy
Sir Al
Judy
Ray
Kenny
Gertrude
Sheila
Sir Garfield
Bridget
Manjusha
Linda
Carolle
Gabriel
Greg
Rosemary
Vincent
Francisco
Maxine
Lady Sharon
Carl R.
Carl
Justov
Sir Paul
Lulu
Rose
007
Sue and Jack

Carrie and Geraldine
Ingrid Hocking
Joseph Figueroa
Hal France
Jennifer Nielsen
David Kitto
Lady Sandra
Antonette
Elizabeth
Reggie Jackson
Michele Roth
Arthur Zbozien
Lady Margaret
Debbie
David Kulowiec
James Copeland
Jennifer W.
Junior Brown
Andrew Shotts
Mr. Perez
Lady Georgia
Sir Brian
Mr.Filipi and family
Michael David
My Angel Virginia
Lady Shannell
Leroy Hernandez
Patricia Shay
Mick Wanamak
Dennis and Sally
Cathy Melichar

Peter Lapina
Annette Zambrana
Tim Garry
Seralie and Alfie
Pat Goldstein
Leslie Torres
Miss X
Punchy
Sam
Donald
Nina
Robert
Marion Oppelt
Tamika
Keith
Black
Lawana
Harry
Art Okun
Stacy King
Charlie Brown
Phyllis Susen
Woody Allen
John Toth
Mr. Wall Street
T.J. Anthony & Joey
Lawyer Andrew Jacobs
Officer Martin, Chanae
Dr. Jacqueline Sawyer
Tamara Wick & Cedric
Monica and Denise
Kyle, his wife and Dakota
Mack the Saxophone Player
Lou and Son – N.Y.P.D.

Sister Saint
Mark
Buffy
Kim Gibbons
Ron Nerain
Bounce
Jelly
Cookie
Joe
Cynthia
Laurie
Curtis
Speedy
Mildred H.
Regina
Mannie
Lynn W.
Jake
Donna
Rebecca
Christine
Arlene
Charlotte
Patricia Best
Jeff
Guy

Clarice Gardner
Sabrina
Vinnie Arrig
Jennifer Gordon
Jeff and Sister
Clint and Bo
Katie
Joni
Christine Resume
Thelma
Johnny
Lydia
Deborah Walker
James Greer
Kristin
George & Christine
Horse
Judge Harold Baer
Ellen Horaitis
Mr. G. and Family
Natalie
Dr. Robert Gibbs
Dr. Barbara Justic
Gabe and Mary Sarah
Mechell & Tamika
Rock and Roll Station D.J.
Reverend Charles and Susan
Donna
Lakeisha
Bonny
Bobby
Adele
Pamela
Jennifer White

157

WBLS Station
57th and Broadway Newsstand Man
57th and 7th Avenue Newsstand Lady
Mr. and Mrs. Michael Sullivan and Ginger
Students at Riverside Elementary School
Times Square Church
New York Urban League
Riverside Church
Abyssinian Church
Covenant Avenue Baptist Church
Gary Byrd, WLIB AM
Victor T. Jones

Judge Kramer and his Legal Staff as well as all the other 9 to 5
lawyers, C.E.O.'s and clerical workers with whom I have come into
contact.

*This space is reserved especially for you. If I
didn't include your name, please feel
honored to have my personal signature
under your name in your own book.*

Thank you,
James C. Simmons

Sun Journal (New Bern, North Carolina: May 28, 1959)

"Negro News"

James C. Simmons, son of Louis Simmons and the late Mrs. Sarah Simmons, of 1025 Church Street, was among the more than 100 graduates to receive their bachelor of science degrees from Shaw University in Raleigh last Monday night. The ceremony was witnessed by Simmons' wife, Mrs. Mamie L. Simmons, his father, a brother and his wife, Mr. and Mrs. John T. Simmons. Other relatives and friends also attended the exercises.

While majoring in mathematics at the university, Simmons was elected president of the student body, received an award from the city chapter of Alpha Phi Alpha fraternity for scholarship, was designated as being the best dressed male student of the university, and held many other key positions pertaining to campus life.

The way I see it, if you want the rainbow,
you gotta put up with the rain.
Dolly Parton

Afterword

As this book goes to publication, I keep in touch with J.C. and his children. I continue to be amazed at their strong feelings of love and concern for their father. I try to make it back to New York every couple of months or so to visit with J.C.

My time spent with J.C. was a learning experience for me. Relating to someone who had a unique perception of reality, and finding ways to form a genuine relationship in spite of that, was an ongoing challenge. Many of my feelings surfaced--feelings of anger, frustration, and powerlessness, but once I accepted his reality as his own, I was able to return to genuine compassion. My struggle was a difficult one, but I finally felt at peace with myself.

My hope is that J.C. has learned that it is possible for him to trust others and that his world doesn't have to be an unsafe and harmful place. Recognizing the good in people, acknowledging it, and giving thanks each day for the chance to make a difference in the lives of others--that's what J.C. and I have done together, each in our own special way.

APPENDICES

> This thing of being homeless, it's not working.
> Something is wrong. Why are there so many people without
> homes? Why? In a country like this?
> *Albert Bell*
> *Black Ballet Pioneer*

Appendix A
A Discussion on Homelessness

The incidence of homelessness has risen to such great levels that researchers are looking carefully at the causes, solutions, and preventative measures. Why do people become homeless? Is it the result of poor decision-making or is it related to the effects of the policies implemented by our society? Can we blame the homeless person, inferring that homelessness is a personal choice, a result of poor judgment or irresponsible behavior? The American work ethic, the belief that hard work guarantees success, places the responsibility on the individual and ignores the circumstances that resulted in homelessness, as well as the economics and policies in society.

Explanations for Homelessness

Jobs

The unemployment rate is the lowest it has been in twenty years. But job opportunities for low-skilled workers have declined.[47] Without further education or job training, many workers will never have a comfortable life. Research shows that welfare recipients move in and out of low paying jobs that cannot support a household and they need education to earn better wages.[48]

Low-skilled workers are making only minimum wage, not enough to successfully support a family. A person would have to work 87 hours a week or find a job that pays $13.00 an hour to afford an apartment at 30% of his income, the standard requirement of banks making mortgage loans.[49]

Homelessness and poverty are linked--when you are poor, you have to prioritize childcare, food, housing, and medical needs. More than one third of those living in poverty have no health insurance so one accident, illness or lost job can result in homelessness. When there is little money, housing is the first to go because it frequently takes up about a half of one's income (U.S.Census, 1998).

Housing

Affordable housing is no longer available to people in a lower-income bracket. Low wages and high-cost housing have created a situation where hard-working Americans cannot afford a place to live. How did this happen?

- Low-rent units disappeared from the housing market and were converted into condominiums, expensive apartments, or just abandoned.

- The demand for low-rent apartments increased but the availability of units decreased.[50]

- Between 1973 and 1993, 2.2 million low-rent units disappeared from the housing market while the demand increased by 4.7 million units.[51]

- There has been a decline of S.R.O.'s because of application of building codes and urban renewal.[52]

163

- The strong economy is worsening the housing crisis for the nation's poorest families as rents increase faster than income.[53]

- Public assistance does not guarantee relief from poverty and homelessness. Applicants must wait anywhere from two to three years for public housing because the number of the people on the waiting list has increased. Only 27% of eligible low-income households are being served. Both time and number of people on the waiting lists for section 8 and public housing have increased since 1996.[54]

- According to the 1998 survey by the International Gospel Mission, 25% of 1,325 heads of homeless families lost their welfare benefits last year.[55]

- One in two homeless families raised in single-parent families or foster care." December 23, 1998. According to the Homes for the Homeless (New York), almost half of welfare recipients in ten cities became homeless between September 1997 and September 1998 after their benefits were reduced or eliminated.[56]

- Benefit levels need to be raised to reflect the cost of housing. According to the New York Times, an appellate court ruled that state officials do not provide welfare recipients enough money to cover rent for an apartment in New York City. A family of 3 receives $286 a month for rent, a sum that has remained unchanged since 1988.[57] It can be concluded that more people are at a greater risk of becoming homeless.

- In a 1998 study by Homes for the Homeless, 22% of 777 women said they had to choose between homelessness or abusive relationships.[58]

Shelters: A Solution?

According to the 1998 United States Conference of Mayors Report, 29 major cities, the homeless outnumber shelter beds.[59] The United States Mayors Report found that in 53% of the cities surveyed, families sometimes have to break up in order to be sheltered. In 50% of the cities, families had to spend daytime hours outside of shelter they use at night.[60]

Homeless individuals feel demoralized in a shelter, having no privacy to change clothes or wash up. The lockers, if available, are easily broken into, so clients must sleep with their belongings close by.[61] Shelters are dirty and chaotic. There is a constant fear of theft, assaults, and sexual advances. Although shelters provide housing, homeless people depend on them for food and clothing also, making it possible for them to spend what little money they have on drugs.

Mental Illness

Deinstitutionalization, the release of long-term mental health patients from psychiatric institutions, was once thought to be responsible for homelessness. In the 1960's and 1970's, deinstitutionalization resulted in a rise in homelessness because community support programs were ill equipped to help the released patients. In addition, individuals who would have normally been institutionalized were remaining in the community.[62]

They needed support in finding housing, medical treatment, and other support. The state and local governments failed to provide this. High caseloads limited medication management and monitoring, in spite of the fact that many had substance abuse problems.

In the 1980's, however, the problem of homelessness exacerbated, not because of deinstitutionalization but because of the decrease of affordable housing. Where were these individuals with psychological problems supposed to live? Mentally ill individuals frequently engage in unpredictable behaviors that threaten themselves or others. Housing stability is jeopardized by delinquent or missing rent payments and neglected maintenance or cleanliness of their apartments, resulting in eviction. In addition, personality characteristics such as isolation and difficulty relating to others can increase their risks of becoming homeless.[63]

There hasn't been an increase of individual problems but rather a decrease in providing assistance to them. For example, many families were dropped from welfare rolls because of new federal mandates and relied instead on emergency providers for food.[64]

In the International Gospel Mission survey, 51% of heads of homeless families were single females, raised in a single parent home, by relatives, or in foster homes. The reasons for homelessness were drugs, alcohol, moving, lost jobs, poor money management, and family breakup.[65]

Current Research

Research shows that certain programs seem to work in helping to eradicate the problem of homelessness.

Affordable Housing
Increased subsidies are needed to make existing housing affordable and create additional, affordable housing.[66]

Health Care
Many jobs do not offer medical benefits. Many people are also losing public assistance and no longer have health insurance.[67] Diseases such as tuberculosis, AIDS, and hepatitis are related to homelessness, yet the homeless aren't getting the necessary treatment.[68]

Employment
Access to job training and education programs that result in jobs providing a living wage are necessary.[69] Lack of a fixed address,

phone number, lack of proper identification and a multitude of other employment obstacles make finding employment difficult.

Supportive Services

Mental health services, substance abuse services, transportation and childcare are needed. The existing networks of support and friendship need to be built upon, enabling homeless individuals to be integrated back into the community. Social work services, including group and individual counseling, are crucial in helping the homeless person resolve personal problems that are impeding his success.[70]

Prevention

The easiest way to help someone is rental assistance. Many times one only needs help for a single month in order to remain in housing. Assistance needs to be equally given to single adults as well as families.[71]

Conclusions

Some people are forced into homelessness by circumstances beyond their control. No one is immune to accidents, deaths in the family, poor financial management or any of the other hundreds of factors that can lead to homelessness.

But the two trends that are largely responsible for the rise in homelessness over the past 15-20 years--poverty and lack of housing--need to be addressed or the underclass of America will continue to be isolated.

A quote from Andrew Cuomo summarizes the actions necessary to deal with homelessness.

"We need to work with Congress to get funding to expand our programs to create more affordable permanent housing, more job training, more substance abuse treatment, more mental health services. Study after study has shown that those programs work and can break the cycle of homelessness."[72]

Volunteers can touch people with their humanity. Heart touches heart, touch brings solace, kindness, cheer and acknowledgment. And the world needs more acknowledgment.

Unknown

Appendix B

Afterthoughts: What Can We Do?

"I was noticed and pulled back up to a place where I could be proud again. Through the efforts of a few people, I was able to get together enough resources to get off the streets. These people gave from their hearts unconditionally, donating their time and money. Along with the many others that donated to me each day, I could now stand tall again. I could tell from the look in their eyes that they wanted to do more, but just didn't know where to begin."

J.C. Simmons.

People do want to help in some way; they just don't know where to begin. The first step is to make the decision to act, to do something to help. After that, it's just a matter of focusing your energies, strengths, and resources. Begin by reading newspaper and magazine articles about the homeless, listening to the news, and contacting organizations and request their brochures, pamphlets, and volunteer needs. Knowledgeable people are better equipped to make informed choices. A great deal of information can be found in the library, bookstores, as well as online. Appendix C lists names and addresses of agencies, web sites, and books.

Individual Advocacy

Advocacy, working to change policies and programs at the local, state, and federal levels is critical to ending homelessness. Individual advocacy is a commitment of one's time and resources to help a specific homeless person.

How a Homeless Person Might React

One of the most emotionally damaging aspects of homelessness is the lack of respect experienced by homeless people in their dealings with individuals and agencies. Trust is a very important issue to the homeless because they typically have lead lives that have been characterized by letdowns and disappointments. The essence of trust is that one can be counted on to keep their commitments. Trust also develops when the homeless person feels like you accept their uniqueness, respect their ability to make decisions, and you communicate genuine concern for them. Simply listening empathetically and intently to the individual can make a huge difference in how the individual perceives herself/himself. Treating the homeless nonjudgmentally and with respect is a good place to begin building a relationship. If they see that you still have hope in them, they will begin to have hope in themselves.

It takes time for a relationship based on trust to develop. Respect each person's boundaries and ways of relating. When you have developed rapport with a homeless individual, you can decide to what extent you want to and are able to help them. Explain to them that you would like to offer your assistance, but it is ultimately up to them. Your assistance may be as simple as offering to get them some clean clothes, or it may entail setting up a job interview for them.

Homeless people react differently to someone's help. Sometimes a homeless person may respond defensively because they feel powerless, and may overreact to try to maintain some control over their situation by being angry and hostile before the other person could. Or they may have repressed their emotions so that when someone helps them, they just accept it numbly without showing appreciation.

A homeless person just wants to be recognized, not ignored. Just making eye contact, smiling or saying hello makes such a difference. Acknowledging one's humanity is one small, yet easy, way to help the homeless.

Steps to Individual Advocacy

■ Step 1 Observing

Begin noticing the homeless people you see on the streets. Keep a journal about who you see, where and when you see them. Take it all in--after awhile you will see the same people at the same places--that's their turf. Notice their appearances and behaviors. Are they: quiet, loud, clean, dirty, male, female, polite, rude, old, young, white, black, thin, heavy, sober, alert, handicapped, busy, listless?

Are they: panhandling, collecting cans, sleeping, drinking, standing, smiling, searching trash, smoking cigarettes, moving around, incoherently talking, singing, yelling, covered with blankets, pushing shopping carts, sleeping on cardboard, dressed warmly?

Regardless of how you decide to help, it is important to be aware of your own feelings and determine if you are open to understanding the homeless. Notice what feelings are stirred up inside you when you approach a homeless person. Are you fearful, disgusted, annoyed, or angry? Do you feel pity or sadness? Do you cross the street to avoid him or her? Do you react differently to a man than a woman, or to someone who is old or young? Do you stop and give him or her change or talk to them? As you walk away, do you feel a sense of relief or a sense of guilt? Do you think about it later?

■ **Step 2   Rely on yourself**

Rely on your gut feeling and decide whom to approach, without jeopardizing your safety. Remember to talk to individuals only in public areas and don't give out any personal information.

Give some change to panhandlers and observe their responses. Stop and talk casually for a few moments, all the time mentally collecting data. Once you've earned someone's trust, begin to ask questions without being too intrusive. Evaluate not only the neediness of each person, but also the potential. You have to have the time to develop a relationship with a homeless person, and this can be done in just a few moments a day.

■ **Step 3   Ask Questions and Develop a Plan**

·   Where do you get your meals?

·   Do you have a favorite food?

·   What clothes do you need that you can't easily get?

·   What do you like to read? Bring magazines, newspapers, and books

·   What kind of music do you like? Bring a small radio or cassette player and tapes.

·   Do you play an instrument? A homeless person who plays an instrument might love getting a guitar, harmonica, or saxophone.

Here are some things you can do:

·   Take someone out to eat--a self-serve deli, a cafe, vendor food, a restaurant.

·   Buy gift certificates to restaurants, or grocery stores.

·   Buy needed clothes, especially cold weather items.

·   Take someone to a shoe store to get a pair of properly fitting shoes.

171

- Give laundry detergent and change for the laundromat.

- Bring a blanket, quilt, sleeping bag, or pillow.

- Pay for a room at a hotel for a shower and a comfortable night's sleep.

- Make a toiletry kit in a practical carrying case. Include band-aids, Tylenol, deodorant, shampoo, razors, shaving cream, tampons, lotion, hand cream, cologne, toothpaste, mouthwash, and "no rinse" soap.

- Take someone to get a haircut or shave, hair color or perm

- Purchase a sketchbook, markers, paints, colored pencils, spiral notebooks, pen, pencils, writing paper, envelopes, and stamps

- Get tickets for cultural events

- Buy subway tokens or a metro card

- Buy a duffel bag, suitcase on wheels, backpack, fanny pack, or umbrella.

- Offer to pay for long-distance phone calls on holidays so they can contact family or friends.

■ Step 4   A Further Commitment

- Some homeless individuals need help obtaining identification. Help write necessary letters, make phone calls, or fill out forms.

- Help may be needed hooking someone up to agencies that could help them. What benefits are they receiving or not receiving and are entitled to? Appendix C lists the agencies and organizations and describes some of their services and in some cases, the name of a contact person.

- Someone may need help with bus or subway fare, finding the location on a map, or calling and making appointments. Go with them, if possible, as their advocate. In addition, they may have too many belongings to travel with (i.e. shopping cart) and ask you to store their items for them.

- Are there any health problems that need to be addressed? Where can these services be obtained? Health problems could include psychological needs as well. You can make necessary phone calls and help get this individual the necessary treatment. Help them get prescriptions filled and manage their dispensing schedule.

■ Step 5   Your Skills and Available Resources

What skills and connections do you have that might help this individual secure housing or employment? Are you in a position to help them financially or offer them a job? Even when someone secures housing, setting up housekeeping can be overwhelming, and help is appreciated in purchasing furniture, kitchen items, and linens as well as arranging for utilities, mail, trash pickup, and keys.

When it is not Possible to Help

But also be careful, realizing that many of the homeless are addicted to drugs, alcohol or are mentally ill. Be cautious in associating with seriously mentally ill persons, chronic alcohol or drug abusers, overly aggressive (verbal or nonverbal) persons and anyone who you do not feel comfortable with.

Whatever you do is important because you are making a contribution to making this world a better place! You are their support; you help them focus; you help keep them positive; you boost their self-esteem and confidence!

> The only way round is through.
> *Robert Frost*

Appendix C
Homeless Resources

Organization/Agency (United States)

American Red Cross
Seventeenth and D Streets NW
Washington D.C. 20006
www.redcross.org

Habitat for Humanity
Habitat and Church Streets
Americus, GA 31709
www.habitat.org
Habitat for Humanity is a nonprofit Christian housing organization building simple, decent, affordable housing in partnership with people in need. Volunteers and partner families provide most of the labor, and individual and corporate donors provide money and materials to build Habitat for Humanity houses.

Health Care for the Homeless
www.amsa.org/programs/homeless
Go to the Homeless Information Center
Newsletter: Opening Doors

National Alliance to End Homelessness

www.end homelessness.org/

Publication: *A Status Report on Hunger and Homelessness in American Cities* (U.S. Conference of Mayors). Excellent source for updates on current policies and legislation. *Newsletter: Alliance*

National Coalition for the Homeless

www.nch.ari.net

The National Coalition for the Homeless is a national advocacy network of homeless persons, activists, service providers, and others committed to ending homelessness through public education, policy advocacy, grassroots organizing, and technical assistance. *Newsletter: Safety Network*

National Health Care for the Homeless Council

www.nhchc.org/

Go to policy and advocacy. Excellent update and recommendations on current projects and legislation, and summaries of current concerns.

National Housing Institute

www.nhi.org

More detailed resources for your perusal! Read the interviews with government officials. *Newsletter: Shelterforce.*

National Law Center on Homelessness and Poverty

www.nlchp.org/

Litigation, legislation and public education information about the homeless and a list of publications to order. Newsletter: *In Just Time.*

National Low Income Housing Coalition

www.nlihc.org/

Becoming knowledgeable about housing is crucial to understanding the problem of homelessness. Publications: *"Out of Reach: Rental Housing at What Cost?"* Go to "Frequently Asked Questions about Housing" for some informative explanations about housing policy.

Salvation Army
615 Slaters Lane Box 269
Alexandria, VA 22314
  www.salvation-army.org
Provides homes to more than 35,000 people throughout the year.
More than 2000 food distribution centers have been operated in the
past year, and more than 2.5 million families are helped in year
through family welfare aid.

U.S. Department of Labor
  www.dol.gov/
Go to "Statistical Data" and "News Releases" for current data on
unemployment, wages, and more.

U.S. Department of Housing and Urban Development (HUD)
  www.hud.gov/
Go to the reading room --Bookshelf 6
Publication: *Waiting in Vain: Update on America's Rental Housing
Crisis*

U.S. Department of Health and Human Services
  www.dhhs.gov/
Go to National Resource Center on Homelessness and Mental
Illness. Excellent source for journal abstracts. *Newsletter: Access.*

Organizations and Agencies (New York City)

Bailey House
275 Seventh Avenue, 12th Floor
New York, NY 10001
212-633-2500
Contact: Siovhan McCloskey, Volunteer Coordinator
www.baileyhouse.org
Bailey House is the second oldest AIDS organization in New York City and serves over two hundred clients a year providing counseling, supportive housing, case management and job training. Many volunteer activities are available. Check out web site for detailed information.

Bowery Mission
227 Bowery
New York, NY 10002
212-674-3456
www.bowery@aol.com

Catholic Charities-New York
1011 First avenue
New York, NY 10022
212-371-1000
www.ny-archdiocese.org
Provides many shelters for the homeless.

Coalition for the Homeless
29 Chambers Street
New York, NY 10007
212-964-5900
www.coalitionforhomeless.org
The nation's oldest and most progressive advocacy and service organization that helps over 2,000 homeless individuals each day.

City Harvest
City Harvest is the only food delivery service in New York City that supplies emergency food programs with deliveries of food on a steady basis of at least once a week. Donated food is matched to the needs of member food programs.

Homes for the Homeless
36 Cooper Square, 6th floor
New York, NY 10003
212-529-5252
Contact: Rebecca Miller
www2.HomesfortheHomeless.com
Founded in 1986, the largest single provider of transitional housing in New York City, serving over 530 homeless families in four different residential education and employment training centers

New York Cares
116 East 16th Street
New York, NY 10003
212-228-5000
www.ny.cares.org.
Each month, over 2,500 volunteers participate in 200 New York projects such as tutoring children, feed the hungry, assist people with aids and much more. Volunteers sign up for an orientation session and then choose from volunteer opportunities.

Salvation Army
Food and Hunger Hot line
212-533-7600

Web Sites

Homeless Education Kit
www.thecity.sfsu.edu/bahp/homeless
Excellent source of information to use in the education of people about homelessness.

Homeless Online
www.homeless.org/
Good link to homeless resources online.

Homeless People's Network Archives
www.asain.asu.edu/
Excellent source of information and discussions about homelessness.

International Homeless Discussion List and Archives
www.csf.colorado.edu/homeless/index.html
Links to over 450 sites with information on the homelessness. Probably one of the best sites to go to and spend hours!

Partnership for the Homeless
www.partnershipforhomeless.org/
Good related links about homelessness.

The Poor People's Guide
www.angelfire.com/or/poor peoples guide/index.html
Good links to obtaining lots of information!

Tedrico's Page Homelessness Resource Links
www.homeless.hypermart.net/
Excellent site containing information on shelters, soup kitchens, panhandling, how to help the homeless and more. User friendly site--developed by homeless man.

Books

Baumohl, Jim. *Homelessness in America* (Oryx Press, 1996).

Burns, Bobby and Snow, David A. *Shelter: One Man's Journey from Homelessness to Hope* (University of Arizona Press, 1998).

Elliott, Michael. *Why the Homeless Don't Have Homes and What to Do About it* (Cleveland, OH: The Pilgrim Press, 1993).

Desjanais, Robert. *Shelter Blues: Sanity and Selfhood Among the Homeless (University of Pennsylvania Press,* 1997).

Dordick, Gwendolyn A. *Something Left to Lose. Personal Relations and Survival Among New York's Homeless* (Philadelphia, PA: Temple University Press, 1997).

Jilner, John. *Sleeping with the Mayor, A True Story.* (St. Paul, Minnesota: John Jilter Hazy Mind Press, 1997).

Kozol, Jonothan. *Rachel and her Children (New York: Random House, 1988).*

Kroloff, Charles A. *54 Ways You Can Help the Homeless* (Connecticut: Lauter Levin Associates Inc.and Behram House, 1993).

Liebow, Elliot. *Tell them Who I am: The Lives of Homeless Women* (New York: Free Press, 1993).

Min, Eungjun. *Reading the Homeless—The Media's Image of Homeless Culture* (Westport, Connecticut: Praeger Publishers, 1999).

The National Alliance to End Homelessness. *What You Can Do to Help the Homeless* (New York: Simon and Schuster, by The Philip Lief Group, Inc. 1991).

Passaro, Joanne. *The Unequal Homeless: Men in the Streets, Women in their Place* (New York: Routledge, 1996).

Pugh, Deborah, and Tietjen, Jeanie. *I Have Arrived Before My Words: The Autobiographical Writings of Homeless Women* (Charles River Press, 1997).

Roleff, Tamara L. *The Homeless--Opposing Viewpoints.* San Diego, California: Greenhaven Press, 1996.

Rossi, Peter H. *Down and Out in America: The Origins of Homelessness.* (Chicago: University of Chicago Press, 1989).

Stringer, Lee. *Grand Central Winter* (New York, NY: Seven Stories Press, 1998).

Vanderstaay, Steven. *Street Lives: An Oral History of Homeless Americans* (Philadelphia, Pennsylvania: New Society Publishers, 1992.

Wright, James D. *Beside the Golden Door: Policy, Politics and the Homeless* (Hawthorne, New York: Aldine de Gruyter, 1998).

Footnotes

Chapter 1

1. Persons with mental illness may show extreme paranoia, anxiety, depression or hallucinations. Approximately 20-25% of the single adult homeless population suffers from some form of severe and persistent mental illness but only 5% who have a serious mental illness are homeless at any given time (*Outcasts on Main Street: A Report of the Federal Task Force on Homelessness and Severe Mental Illness,* 1992).

Chapter 2

2. The most widely estimate is approximately 500,000 to 600,000 homeless people (Burt and Cohen, 1989). This number is updated to allow a 5% increase a year resulting in an estimate of over 700,000 and up to two million people who experience homelessness during one year. The National Coalition for the Homeless estimate 760,000 homeless people are on the streets, fifty percent more than were counted in 1988 (*National Law Center of Homelessness and Poverty, 1999*). There are over 40,000 homeless people in New York City. More than 23,000 New Yorkers sleep in homeless shelters each night (Andrew Hsiar, "The Disappeared," *Village Voice*, December 8, 1998). In addition, in 19 major cities, the homeless outnumber the number of shelter beds (John Bacon, "Aggressive beggars now a no-no in New York City," *USA Today*, September 27, 1996:3A).

3. Despite the difficulty determining the incidence of homelessness, the *U. S. Conference of Mayors Report* (December, 1998) states that children account for 25% of the homeless population; families with children account for 38% of the homeless population; single adult men account for 45%. Out of this group, 22% are veterans.

4. Many people with mental illness have difficulty developing and maintaining comfortable social relationships. This can lead to loneliness and isolation, as well as conflicts with landlords and neighbors. These conflicts can result in homelessness if appropriate treatment and services are not available (*Federal Task Force on Homelessness and Mental Illness*, 1992).

5. Poverty is increasing because of decreasing job opportunities and the declining value and availability of public assistance. In 1997, 36.9 million people (13.3%) in the United States lived in poverty and almost half of those lived in extreme poverty (*U.S.Census,* 1998). The economic reality of America is that the very rich are getting richer and the very poor, poorer. From 1970 to 1997, the income of the top 5% increased while the income of the lowest 20% decreased (Deborah Stone, "The Homeless," *The New Republic,* Volume 210, June 27, 1994: 29).

6. *U. S. Conference of Mayors Report.* "A Status Report on Hunger and Homelessness in American Cities, December, 1998.

7. Persons with mental illness are at particular risk for substance abuse. The substance abuse starts while they are homeless. In many cases, substance abuse precedes an individual's loss of regular housing and can be considered a primary cause of his homeless condition (*National Law Center on Homelessness and Poverty,* January, 1999).

8. In a number of cities not surveyed, the percentage was even higher (*National Coalition for the Homeless,* 1997).

Chapter 4

9. Crime in the subway dropped from 487 to 394 incidences of grand larceny during the first two months of 1997 and 1998. Credit is due to the fact that the "police and people are doing a better job of looking after one another." In addition, police report

a significant drop in the first four months of 1999 (Thomas J. Lueck, "Crime in the Subways Declines Again," *New York Times*, May 18, 1999).

Chapter 5

10. Many newspaper articles about drugs concerned the 34th, 73rd and 94th precincts. "Federal law enforcement officials are investigating allegations of drug-dealing by groups of police officers in one of New York City's most violent, drug-ridden precincts and suspect that there are pockets of corrupt officers in several other precincts"(Craig Wolff, "U.S. is Investigating Reports of Corrupt New York Police," *New York Times,* June 19, 1992: A1).

Chapter 6

11. The nation's oldest and most progressive advocacy and service organization, the Coalition serves over 2000 homeless persons each day in obtaining housing, food, job training, clothing, and other vital services *National Coalition for the Homeless (NCH),* http://www. nch.ari.net.

12. Results from the national survey from the Monitoring the Future Study of American secondary students state that illicit drug use by this age group is heading down after six years of steady increases ("Monitoring the Future Study Press Release, *University of Michigan Institute for Social Research,* December 18, 1998).

13. A study in 1996 stated, "Of the country's largest cities, 19 had initiated crackdowns on the homeless in the mid-1990's. Twenty-seven had recently engaged in police sweeps of homeless people (*National Law Center on Homelessness and Poverty,* 1996). A study in 1999 states, "There continues to be a crackdown on homeless people. As the mayor focuses on quality of life violations, sweeps continue on almost a daily basis."

("Cities cold-hearted when dealing with the homeless," *National Law Center on Homelessness and Poverty*, January 8, 1999).

14. St. Patrick's Cathedral--Resource List for Homeless Persons

15. According to the 1999 figures, the National Coalition for the Homeless reported that the number of S.R.O.apartments decreased by 87% in New York City. Progress and urban renewal eliminated the single-room occupancy hotels where many addicts and mentally ill on the streets lived—the original "skid row" hotels are long gone, replaced by boutiques, cafes and clubs (Laura Parker, "Homeless find the Streets Growing Colder," *USA Today*, December 3, 1998:15A).

16. *U.S. Conference of Mayors Report*, "A Status Report on Hunger and Homelessness in American Cities," December, 1998.

17. Benefit levels need to be raised to reflect the cost of housing. According to the New York Times, an appellate court ruled that state officials do not provide welfare recipient enough for an apartment in New York City. A family of 3 receives $286 a month for rent, a sum that has remained unchanged since 1988. It can be concluded that more people are at a greater risk of becoming homeless (Rachel L. Swarns, "Court Finds Welfare Pays Too Little for Rent," *The New York Times,* May 7, 1999: B3).

18. Some of the programs that have been successful include those under The Department of Health and Human Services (i.e. PATH, ACCESS, Runaway and Homeless Youth Project, SSI Outreach Project). Other successful services are provided by: Bailey House, Strive, Homes for the Homeless, Project for Psychiatric Outreach to the Homeless, Coalition for the Homeless-NewYork/NewYork Agreement, Housing Works, Inc. and Project Renewal.

19. The Clinton Administration spent $5 million on the homeless between 1987-1993, most of it going to the "continuum of care" programs that provide temporary housing, counseling, and job training. This approach has been successful for some but advocates still believe that affordable housing has to increase in order for homelessness to end (Romesh Ratnesar, "Nation, Not Gone, but Forgotten? Why Americans have stopped talking about homelessness," *Time Inc.,* February 8, 1999: pp 30+).

"A number of outreach programs have helped many homeless with serious mental illnesses. However, the cost to run these programs is high and more case management is needed. Most homeless people with mental illness receive minimal treatment and services and go in and out of hospitals, jails, shelters and life on the streets."(*National Resource Center on Homelessness and Mental Illness).*

Chapter 8

20. Midnight Run, a nonprofit group that takes food and clothing to the homeless, has volunteers from over 100 churches, synagogues and schools in Westchester County in New York (Roberta Hershenson, "Group Aiding Homeless to Get Concert Funds," *New York Times,* XIII, March 27, 1996: p.11).

21. "In interviews with more than two dozen New Yorkers who say they give money to panhandlers, a recurring theme is trust. Some, worrying about being robbed, scan their surroundings before pulling out their wallets. Others say they want to be sure that the person really needs the money, so they give to people whose clothes look tattered or look honest" (Emily Bernstein, "Quarter, Quarter, Dollar? Sidewalk Charity Lives," *New York Times,* July 27, 1993: B3).

22. *The Bay Area Homeless Alliance* (BAHA) is a collaboration of Service agencies in San Francisco. They work to prevent or reduce homelessness. This web site (http://www.baha.org/) provides information and referral to individuals or agencies. The

BAHA has recently been commended by the U.S. Department of Housing and Urban Development (HUD) for "outstanding performance in meeting the needs of the homeless .."

Chapter 9

23. In order to obtain a shelter bed, you have to be determined eligible. If you aren't eligible, you reapply the next day. If you are eligible, you wait for your name to be called, and then you are shuttled from shelter to shelter, trying to find an open bed. If you find one, your sleep is interrupted in the early morning (5:00 am) and you are taken back to the Intake Center to wait in line for a bed for the next night. Some people will just sleep in chairs or on the floor of the intake center to avoid this grueling process. This intake process, however time-consuming and demeaning, must be done in order to enter into the shelter system (Randy Kennedy, "For Homeless in From the Cold, a Shuffled from Site to Site," *New York Times,* January 29, 1997: B1 and Robert Polner, "Charity Group Decry Policies," *Newsday,* October 13, 1998: p. 43).

24. "A person gets tired sleeping on the street. Men are lucky to get a shelter bed once or twice a month. Women fare a little better with a couple nights a week. After awhile you need to sleep in a real bed . . . but you don't have money for a hotel room" (Panhandling: A Little Understanding, an article reprinted from *San Francisco's Street Sheet, A Publication of the Coalition on Homelesness,* San Francisco, December, 1997).

25. A shelter is frequently run like a correctional facility, with numerous rules and regulations, including what time to get up, when to wait in line for food, when to shower, and what bed to sleep in. This kind of environment can undermine self-esteem. "There's a culture of violating clients' rights and disrespect for them. It's like a jail" (Michael O'Malley, "Homeless Say Shelters Badly Run," *Cleveland Plain Dealer,* May 29, 1999:C29).

26. Workfare is a general term that refers to any program that requires recipients of public assistance to work for a public agency in order to receive benefits. New York City's version of workfare, called the Work Experience Program (WEP) was implemented in 1995 (Eric Snyder, "Workfare Punishes Homeless in New York City," *New York Times*).

27. There is a high risk for tuberculosis in shelters. Homelessness is a public health crisis. Diseases such as tuberculosis, aids, and hepatitis are related to homelessness yet the homeless aren't getting the necessary treatment (Gelberg, L. "Tuberculosis Skin Testing among Homeless Adults," *Journal of Internal Medicine,* Vol. 12, 1997: 25-33 and Parker, Laura, "Homeless Finding the Streets Growing Colder," *USA Today,* December 3, 1998: 15A).

Chapter 10

28. The New York State Office of Drug Abuse estimates that in New York City on any given day as many as 150,000 people are selling and distributing crack. Crack continues to rise among teenagers, middle class adults and former heroin addicts. (Terry Williams, *Crackhouse: Notes from the End of the Line.* (Penguin Books, 1993: pp 1-23). The highest rates of illicit drug use are found among youth ages 16-17 and 18-20 with marijuana being the most common drug. In addition, young people do not perceive crack as a risk. However, this perception is declinging among upper grades and leveling off with eighth graders (National Institute of Drug Abuse, Monitoring the Future Study Press Release, December 18, 1998).

29. Michael T. Kaufman, "A Middleman's Venture in the Can Trade," *New York Times,* September 23,1992: A1.

Chapter 11

30. "The problem is getting worse because we are addressing at the level of symptoms, blaming homeless for their behavior, getting angry at the presence of homelessness and homeless people. We are dealing with homelessness as if it were a choice. If it's a choice, then why are people making such poor choices?" (The Bay Area Homeless Program).

31. ". . . homeless people prefer private shelters and even the streets than to take shelter for the night at either the Franklin shelter in the Bronx or the Atlantic Avenue shelter ... those are dangerous places; not fit for humans (Randy Kennedy, "For Homeless in From the Cold, a Shuffled from Site to Site," *New York Times,* January 29,1997).

32. Chapin Wright, "Panel Urges Revamp of Shelters," *Newsday,* February 17, 1992: p.15.

33. Deborah Stone, "The Homeless," *The New Republic,* Volume 210, June 27, 1994: p. 29.

34. Ibid

35. 80% of homeless families that received subsidized apartments had remained intact—out of shelters and off the streets (Nichole M. Christian, "Study Offers New Insight on Homeless," (from American Journal of Public Health), *New York Times*, November 8, 1998: p. 39).

36. "New York's Homeless. On the Edge," *The Economist,* July 6, 1996: pp. 28-29 and Louise Starks, "From Lemons to Lemonade: An Ethnographic Sketch of Late Twentieth-century Panhandling," *New England Journal of Public Policy,"* 1992, 8/1:341-352.

Chapter 14

37. Do the poor have a right to beg? Yes, according to federal district court judge in New York Circuit of Appeals who ruled in 1993 that New York City could not ban begging on the street because panhandling was a form of free speech, protected by the first amendment (Michael Ybarra, "Don't Ask, Don't Beg, Don't Sit," *New York Times*, May 1996: p. 86). "The first amendment gives individuals the right to food, shelter, and clothing and the right to ask for help and a person conveys this when they hold out their hand for a donation." (Patricia Cohen, "Sidewalk Beggars Win Court Approval for Panhandling," *Newsday,* July 30, 1993: p. 6).

38. The "rules of conduct" at Sony Plaza, a public arcade off Madison Avenue, now seeks to ban visitors carrying "excessive packages." (*The Economist,* "New York's Homeless: On the Edge," July 6, 1996: pp-28-29).

39. In 1996, Mayor Guilliani signed into law an ordinance than banned aggressive panhandling. "Aggressive" panhandling, punishable by up to 16 days in jail and a $100 fine, includes blocking a pedestrian or car, using threatening gestures, touching or causing alarm or unreasonable inconvenience (John Bacon, "Aggressive beggars now a no-no in New York City," *USA Today,* September 27, 1996: 3A).

40. *The Bay Area Homeless Alliance* (BAHA)

41. Lynette Lamb, "Compassion Fatigue," *Utne Reader*, July/August 1992: pp 17-18.

42. "Advocates say the crackdown by the New York City Police Department on quality of life crimes in Manhattan is aimed at homeless people. The crackdown, described in an unpublished, internal Police Department memo as "a major initiative aimed at achieving additional improvements in quality of life conditions

in the midtown area," lists offenses like peddling, panhandling and prostitution, along with squeegee wielding, open consumption of alcohol, public urination and ticket scalping. It specifies the area between 30th and 59th Streets, from river to river, although advocates for the homeless say the scope has widened to include everything below 110th Street. The concern is that police will use insignificant situations as sitting on the back of a park bench or spitting to handcuff, fingerprint and check people for outstanding arrest warrants. Panhandling and squeegees are often problems so this crackdown is directed at the homeless." (*National Law Center on Homelessness and Poverty,* January 8, 1999 and Robert Polner, "Quality Control/Advocates Claim Homeless Target of Cop Crackdown, *Newsday,* August 29, 1996: A7)

43. Ellis Henican, "In the Subways Blank stares, Empty Cups for Beggars, *Newsday*, January 27, 1994: p 6.

44. Andrew Hsiar, "The Disappeared," *Village Voice,* December 8, 1998.

45. *The Bay Area Homeless Alliance* (BAHA)

46. Beggar free quotation San Francisco Chronicle, Editorial, March 2, 1996.

Appendix A

47. In New York City, it was 6.5% in March, 1999, down from 8% in 1998 (Leslie Eaton, "City's Unemployment Rate Stays at Its Lowest," *New York Times,* May 5, 1999).

48. *National Coalition for the Homeless,* NCH Fact Sheet #4, February, 1999 and "Vanishing Act," The Progressive, Volume 62, May 1, 1998: p 8.

49. Deborah Stone, "The Homeless," *The New Republic,* Volume 210, June 27, 1994: p. 29.

50. *U. S. Mayors Conference Report,* "A Status Report on Hunger and Homelessness in American Cities," December, 1998.

51. Ibid

52. Andrew Hsiar, "The Disappeared," *Village Voice,* December 8, 1998.

53. Andrew Cuomo, *National Press Club,* "Waiting in Vain: An Update on America's Rental Housing Crisis," April 28, 1999.

54. *National Low Income Housing Coalition,* 1998 and "Vanishing Act," *The Progressive,* Volume 62, May 1,1998: p 8.

55. *International Union Gospel Missions,* "The Changing Face of America's Homeless: IUGM Issues Tenth Annual Survey, November 23, 1998.

56. *Homes for the Homeless,* Study of 777 homeless parent in ten United States cities (1998).

57. Rachel L Swarns, "Court Finds Welfare Pays Too Little for Rent," *The New York Times,* May 7,1999: B3.

58. *Homes for the Homeless*

59. *U. S. Mayors Conference Report, "A Status Report on Hunger and Homelessness in American Cities," December, 1998.

60. Ibid

61. Deborah Stone, "The Homeless," *The New Republic*, Volume 210, June 27,1994: p. 29.

62. Mary Ellen Hombs. *American Homelessness* (Santa Barbara, CA: ABC-CLIO-INC. 1994), p 8.

63. Jencks, Christopher. *The Homeless* (Cambridge, MA: Harvard University Press, 1994).

64. A study by the Center for Poverty Solutions showed 23% more people needed help in obtaining shelter and sustenance in 1998 than 1997. Families dropped from welfare rolls because of new federal mandates turned to emergency providers to feed themselves and their children. *Washington Times,* December 16, 1998: C2.

65. *International Union Gospel Missions,* "The Changing Face of America's Homeless: IUGM Issues Tenth Annual Survey, November 23, 1998. Susan Wright, spokesperson for the city's department of the homeless, shares the view that subsidized housing is an effective way of helping the 4,700 homeless families now living in the city's shelters (*New York Times,* November 1, 1998).

66. *National Law Center on Homelessness and Poverty,* January 8, 1999.

67. *National Coalition for the Homeless (NCH),* Fact Sheet #1, June, 1999.

68. Gelberg, L. "Tuberculosis Skin Testing among Homeless Adults," *Journal of Internal Medicine,* Vol. 12, 1997, p. 25 and Parker, Laura, "Homeless find the Streets Growing Colder," *USA Today,* December 3, 1998: 15A

69. *National Law Center on Homelessness and Poverty,* January 8, 1999.

70. Ibid

71. *National Law Center on Homelessness and Poverty,* January 8, 1999.

72. Andrew Cuomo, "Mayors' Survey Showing Need for Homeless Programs," *U.S. Department of Housing and Urban Development*, December 23, 1998.

Bibliography

Bacon, John. "Aggressive beggars now a no-no in New York City," *USA Today,* September 27,1996.

Bernstein Emily. "Quarter, Quarter, Dollar? Sidewalk Charity Lives On," *New York Times*, July 27, 1993.

Bowen, Elizabeth. "Even Panhandlers Deserve Respect," *University Wire*, November 17, 1998.

Burt, Martha and Cohen, Barb E. *America's Homeless: Numbers, Characteristics, and Programs that Serve Them.* Washington D.C.:Urban Institute Press, 1989.

Cohen, Patricia. "Sidewalk Beggars Win Court Approval for Panhandling," *Newsday,* July 30, 1993.

The Economist, "New York's Homeless. On the Edge," July 6, 1996.

Gelberg, L. "Tuberculosis Skin Testing among Homeless Adults," *Journal of Internal Medicine,* Vol. 12, 1997.

Henican, Ellis. "In the Subways Blank stares, Empty Cups for Beggars," *Newsday*, January 27,1994.

Hemphill, Clara. "New York Forum about Panhandlers Begging Off the Old Job," *Newsday,* October 14, 1992.

Hombs, Mary Ellen. *American Homelessness.* Santa Barbara, California: ABC-CLIO, 1994.

Hsiar, Andrew. "The Disappeared," *The Village Voice,* December 1998.

International Union Gospel Missions, "The Changing Face of America's Homeless: IUGM Issues Tenth Annual Survey, November 23, 1998.

Jencks, Christopher. *The Homeless.* Cambridge, MA: Harvard University Press, 1994.

Kaufman, Michael T. "A Middleman's Venture in the Can Trade," *New York Times,* September 23, 1992.

Kennedy, Randy. "For Homeless in From the Cold, a Shuffled from Site to Site," *New York Times,* January 29, 1997.

Lamb, Lynnette. "Compassion Fatigue," *Utne Reader,* July/August 1992.

Lueck, Thomas J. "Crime in the Subways Declines Again," *New York Times,* May 18, 1999.

O'Malley, Michael. "Homeless Say Shelters Badly Run," *Cleveland Plain Dealer,* May 29, 1999.

National Coalition for the Homeless, http://www.nch.ari.net

National Law Center on Homelessness and Poverty, "Cities Cold-hearted When Dealing with the Homeless," January 8, 1999.

Parker, Laura, "Homeless find the Streets Growing Colder," *USA Today,* December 3, 1998.

Polner, Robert. "Charity Group Decry Policies," *Newsday,* October 13, 1998.

Quindlen, Anna. "No Place Like Home," *New York Times, May 20, 1993.*

Ratnesar, Romesh. "Nation, Not Gone, but Forgotten? Why Americans have stopped talking about homelessness," *Time, Inc.,* February 8, 1999.

Starks, Louise. "From Lemons to Lemonade: An Ethnographic Sketch of Late Twentieth-century Panhandling," *New England Journal of Public Policy,* 1992, 8/1.

Stone Deborah. "The Homeless," *The New Republic,* Volume 210, June 27, 1994.

Swarns, Rachael. "Court Finds Welfare Pays Too Little for Rent," *The New York Times,* May 7, 1999.

United States Conference of Mayors Report. "A Status Report on Hunger and Homelessness in American Cities, December, 1998.

Walsch, Neale Donald. *Conversations with God--Book 3.* Charlottesville, Virginia: Hampton Road Publishing Company, 1998.

Williams, Terry. *Crackhouse: Notes from the End of the Line.* Penguin Books, 1993.

Wolff, Craig. "U. S. is Investigating Reports of Corrupt New York Police," *New York Times,* June 19, 1992.

Ybarra, Michael. "Don't Ask, Don't Beg, Don't Sit," *New York Times,* May 19, 1996.

Zukav, Gary. *The Seat of the Soul.* New York, New York: Simon and Schuster, 1990.

To order additional copies of **Have a Great One! A Homeless Man's Story,** complete the information below.

Ship to:

Name_____

Address_____

City, State, Zip _____

Day Phone _____

___ copies of **Have a Great One! A Homeless Man's Story**

   @ $12.95 each $ _____

Tax   **$1.75 each**   _____

Shipping and Handling **$3.20 each**   _____

             Total Amount Due   _____

Make checks payable to: Laurie Anthony

Send to: Laurie Anthony

P.O. Box 3522 * Dublin, OH 43016